The Torturing Of An American Hero

I ACCUSE

■

By Melinda Stephens

Text Copyright 1987 by Melinda Stephens.

All rights reserved.

Library of Congress Catalog Card Number: 87-70269

American Ideal Publishing

Printed in the United States of America

PREFACE

CHRONOLOGY OF EVENTS 1969–1986

Winter, 1969, to August, 1985, taken from a letter written by Dr. Jeffrey R. Mac-Donald to his supporters, published in Volume 4 of the "MacDonald Newsletter."

JULY, 1969. I enter the U.S. Army after a surgical internship at Columbia-Presbyterian Hospital in New York. My basic training is completed at Fort Sam Houston, Texas. Then I volunteer for Airborne (Paratrooper) training and Special Forces (Green Beret). By early Fall, I am actively engaged in being a "Group Surgeon" for a Special Forces unit at Ft. Bragg, North Carolina, and my family has moved here from New York.

WINTER OF 1969-1970. Colette, Kim, Kristy and I develop a nice life at Ft. Bragg. The strains of medical school and internship, as well as financial hardship, are behind us. Christmas is perhaps our best time together ever, shared with my in-laws at Ft. Bragg.

EARLY MORNING–FEBRUARY 17, 1970. At

least four intruders, probably more, enter our house and brutally murder Colette, Kim and Kristy. I suffer multiple stab and blunt trauma wounds, am left unconscious, and eventually receive two chest tubes to re-expand a partially collapsed lung, while hospitalized at Womack Army Hospital. The Army announces a search for intruders.

LATER ON, FEBRUARY 17, 1970. Three "Chief" Army CID investigators decide between themselves on faulty information and essentially NO interviews, that the crime scene they found was "staged." From that moment on, no real search for the killers ever takes place. I am (secretly) the object of all of their "forensic" and other investigations.

APRIL 6, 1970. I am accused by the U.S. Army CID as a "suspect" of the crimes and confined to quarters though I have never witnessed any line-ups, seen any possible suspects or been interviewed since hospitalization.

MAY 1, 1970. I am publicly accused by the CID as the "chief" suspect and am charged with the crimes, although the CID has to apparently force my commanding officer to prefer charges, because he is confused by the lack of any real evidence.

JULY-OCTOBER 1970. The Army holds an Article 32 Hearing, presided over by a Colonel with a legal officer sitting next to him for legal advice. All pertinent witnesses we are aware of, testify. Helena Stoeckley emerges as a suspect.

The CID either attempts to change forensic reports which point toward my innocence or tries to prevent them from being submitted as evidence.

OCTOBER, 1970. Col. Warren Rock (Article 32 Hearing officer) states the charges "are not true." He lists the reasons in a meticulous and lengthy written report. He specifically deals with the forensic and psychiatric evidence which assists him in making this decision. I am released from custody and returned to duty. The army publicly states the charges were dropped "for lack of evidence" which twists and weakens the actual Article 32 hearing conclusions.

DECEMBER, 1970. I obtain an honorable discharge from the U.S. Army and begin work as a physician in New York prior to my residency at Yale, scheduled to begin in July of 1971. Meanwhile, my father-in-law and myself begin a campaign to have the conduct of the CID investigated and the case itself reinvestigated. Later, we find out this request generated activity in the Justice Department, who eventually asked the CID to investigate itself. The CID re-investigation of itself began in early 1971.

JUNE, 1971. I withdraw from the Yale residency just prior to beginning it and relocate in Long Beach, California, after receiving an offer from my friend, Dr. Jerry Hughes, another ex-Green Beret physician. I am warned by my in-laws that I had "better not" move to the West Coast to rebuild my life. I disregarded this warning and begin to rebuild my life in Long Beach in emergency medicine.

JUNE, 1971. The CID "completes" its re-investigation, which states that the CID was correct in its initial charges against me. No charges are preferred against the investigators who manipulated evidence in 1970. The CID "conclusions" are passed around the U.S. Justice Department for years, with numerous lawyers, one after the other, refusing to prosecute.

AUGUST, 1974. A prior Army investigator in the CID "reinvestigation," Brian Murtaugh, now a civilian lawyer in the Justice Department, reopens the case by arranging for a Grand Jury in Raleigh, North Carolina. The prosecution team is headed by Victor Worheide, a specialist in obtaining indictments in so-called "difficult" prosecutions. The Grand Jury meets for six months until January, 1975, seeing every witness the prosecution presents to buttress their case. No defense, of course, or defense lawyers, are allowed in the Grand Jury room.

JANUARY, 1975. I agree to take a Sodium Amytal (Truth Serum) test for the Grand Jury. The prosecutor prevents the test from occurring. The Grand Jury indicts me in January, 1975.

After the indictment—January, 1975, I am arrested by the FBI, jailed and obtain bail a week later. I return to work and begin re-building a defense team for the upcoming trial. We are very confused, as nothing in the facts of the case has changed from 1970. We file a multitude of pre-trial appeals.

JANUARY, 1976. The 4th Circuit Court of Appeals, from among the appeals we file, finds for me on "Speedy Trial" grounds and all charges are dismissed. I resume the next attempt to rebuild my life and career.

MAY, 1978. The U.S. Supreme Court reverses my appeal win, and orders a trial, saying you can't prevent a trial by claiming speedy trial violations.

JULY, 1979. The trial begins in Raleigh, North Carolina and lasts until August 29, 1979. Judge Dupree refuses all 24 pre-trial and trial motions in regard to evidence, witnesses, etc. Judge Dupree does not allow seven crucial witnesses (who corroborate Helena Stoeckley's admissions of guilt) to testify in front of the jury. In addition, Judge Dupree disallows the psychiatric evidence, the findings of the Article 32 hearings in 1970, and even cuts off character witnesses.

Joe McGinniss enters the case in June of 1979, claiming he will write the true story and claiming he will obtain advance dollars from a publisher that I can use to help defray defense costs.

AUGUST 19, 1979. Guilty verdict. I am sentenced to three consecutive life sentences and prison incarceration begins. Appeals are filed shortly thereafter.

AUGUST 22, 1980. U.S. 4th Circuit Court of Appeals dismisses all charges, overturning the conviction, again choosing the Speedy Trial issue from all of our appeals. I am released from prison to begin rebuilding my life and career again after a year in prison.

MARCH 31, 1982. The Supreme Court again reinstates the conviction, saying my speedy trial rights were not violated. I return to prison within one hour of the Supreme Court decision. Meanwhile, my private investigator during this time, has located Helena Stoeckley and obtained a signed confession about the commission of the crimes.

AUGUST 27, 1982. I am transferred suddenly from Terminal Island, California, to Bastrop, Texas. The move occurs 48 hours after a Jack Anderson TV interview about the new evidence in the case, and three days after retaining a new attorney, Brian O'Neill.

JANUARY 10, 1983. The Supreme Court refused to even hear my appeal based on trial error. My new attorney, Brian O'Neill and new investigator, Ray Shedlick, enter the case and begin to delve into new evidence surrounding Helena Stoeckley's confession. We finally begin to obtain (3-1/2 years after filing the request) government files on my case and discover evidence favorable to me that was either intentionally destroyed or hidden from the defense team, dating all the way back to 1970

SEPTEMBER, 1983. Joe McGinniss publishes "Fatal Vision" and, contrary to what we believed for four years, he has republished and expanded upon, the government mis-information on the case. McGinniss ignores the government misconduct, lost evidence, hidden evidence and new evidence pertaining to my innocence.

APRIL, 1984. The defense files four motions for a new trial, with solid corroborating evidence pointing to my innocence. Newly discovered evidence also proves a major prosecutor in my case was Judge Dupree's son-in-law.

SEPTEMBER, 1984. Fraud and libel suits are filed against Joe McGinniss. New witnesses keep appearing in the case, both with new evidence as to my innocence and verification that "Fatal Vision" is grossly incorrect in its so-called "facts" and "conclusions."

NOVEMBER, 1984. NBC, resisting repeated legal attempts by the defense team to correct errors in the script, airs "Fatal Vision" over our vigorous objections.

MARCH 1, 1985. Judge Dupree, still the judge in the case, refuses to take himself off the case, despite his son-in-law's proven involvement; and denies all motions for a new trial based on new evidence. He completely disregards 35 new witnesses corroborating Helena Stoeckley's confessions. He ignores seven items of previously suppressed evidence favorable to the defense, and he refuses to acknowledge a phoney psychiatric exam by the government investigator designed to prevent legitimate psychiatric testimony.

AUGUST, 1985. Witnesses continue to come forward to rebut the government theory, as well as the conclusions drawn by Joe McGinniss in "Fatal Vision." The defense team finalizes all appeals for the U.S. 4th Circuit Court of Appeals. Oral arguments on the new evidence are scheduled for a day during the week of October 7, in Richmond Virginia. I remain at Bastrop, now having served four years and four months in prison for crimes I did not commit.

DECEMBER, 1986. (Update, continued by the author.) The 4th Circuit Court of Appeals denies MacDonald's motions for a new trial or dismissal of the charges, and days later, MacDonald is suddenly transferred from Bastrop, Texas, to Phoenix, Arizona, by way of El Reno, Oklahoma.

JANUARY, 1986. A petition for a rehearing en banc (by all of the 4th Circuit Court judges) is denied.

MAY, 1986. MacDonald petitions the Supreme Court to hear his case.

SEPTEMBER, 1986. Dr. Thomas T. Noguchi, one of the world's foremost pathologists, declares MacDonald innocent of the murders after an extensive study of the autopsy reports.

OCTOBER 6, 1986. The Supreme Court lets the 4th Circuit Court of Appeals decision stand.

The MacDonald home at Fort Bragg, on Castle Drive,
where the murders took place.

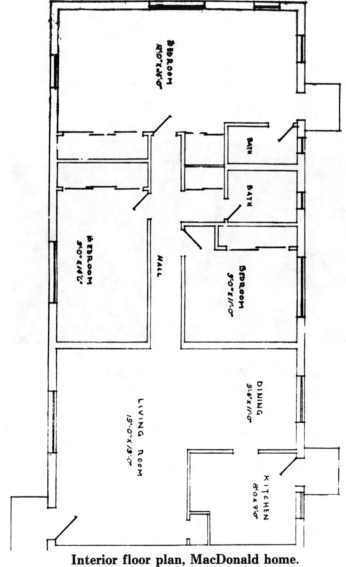

Interior floor plan, MacDonald home.

Fort Bragg information map.

INDEX TO BUILDINGS

1. NORMANDY HOUSE (VISITOR AND PROTOCOL BUREAU)
2. GUEST HOUSE NO. 1
3. GUEST HOUSE NO. 2
4. GUEST HOUSE NO. 4
5. XVIII AIRBORNE & FT. BRAGG HQ
6. XVIII AIRBORNE ARTILLERY HQ
7. 82 DIVISION HQ
8. SPECIAL WARFARE HQ
9. USA GAR., CASUAL BRANCH
10. MATA STUDENT REPORTING STA.
11. MAIN OFFICER'S CLUB
12. MAIN NCO CLUB
13. 82 DIVISION NCO CLUB
14. MAIN E-4 CLUB
15. MAIN PX
16. MALLONEE SHOPPING CENTER

17. MAIN COMMISSARY
18. DRIVE-IN SNACK BAR
19. PX AUTO SERVICE AREA
20. VEHICLE INSPECTION STATION
21. HOUSING OFFICE
22. PROVOST MARSHAL
23. MURRAY SCHOOL
24. BUTNER SCHOOL
25. IRWIN SCHOOL
26. BOWLEY SCHOOL
27. HOLBROOK SCHOOL
28. MC NAIR SCHOOL
29. NURSERY SCHOOL
30. KINDERGARTEN AREA
31. WOMACK HOSPITAL
32. MAIN CHAPEL
33. TELEPHONE AND TELEGRAPH

34. PERSONAL SERVICES (ID AND PRIVILEGE CARDS)
35. RED CROSS
36. POST THEATRES
37. POST PLAYHOUSE
38. POST TRANSPORTATION
39. LEGAL ASSISTANCE
40. MAIN POST LIBRARY
41. PET REGISTRATION
42. RETIRED ACTIVITIES
43. SPECIAL SERVICES OFFICE
44. MAIN POST CRAFT.SHOP
45. QM LAUNDRY
46. LEE FIELD HOUSE
47. HEDRICK STADIUM
48. TOWLE STADIUM
49. STRYKER GOLF COURSE
50. POST RIDING STABLES

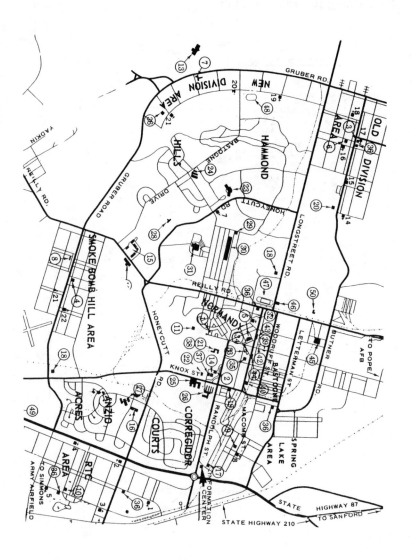

The defense

Brian O'Neill, Esq.......Chief Counsel for the 1984-85 Evidentiary Hearings of the new evidence compiled after the 1979 trial, and the 4th Circuit Court Appeal following these hearings.

Bernard Segal, Esq.......Chief Counsel for the 1970 Army Article 32 Hearings, the 1979 trial and all appeals specifically relating to this trial.

Dennis H. Eisman, Esq....Chief Defense Counsel from fall, 1986, to present. 1986 Writ of Certiorari for the Supreme Court, October term. Amicus Curiae (Friend of the Court brief) for National Association of Criminal Defense Lawyers for the 1985 4th Circuit Court Appeal. Assisted Bernard Segal in 1970 Article 32 Hearing.

Wade Smith, Esq..........Raleigh, North Carolina, lawyer who coordinated closely with Bernard Segal during the 1979 trial and with Brian

O'Neill during the 1984-85 Eviden-
ţiary Hearings.

Michaèl J. Malley, Esq...Army Defense
Counsel for the 1970 Army Article 32
Hearings. Consultant on all legal
matters for MacDonald from 1970 to
the present.

Gary L. Bostwick, Esq....Chief Counsel
for Civil Suit against writer, Joe
McGinniss.

Raymond Shedlick, Sr.....Chief Investigator for Defense and Civil cases
1983 to present.

Dr. John Thornton........Forensics expert, 1979 trial.

Dr. Thomas T. Noguchi....Forensics expert. 1986 to present.

Ted Gunderson ....Chief Investigator from 1980 to 1982

Prince Beasley...........Police Officer
on case in 1970, and Investigator,
1980 to 1982.

MACDONALD'S PROSECUTORS

James Blackburn, Esq.....Assistant United
States Attorney, 1979 trial.

Brian Murtaugh, Esq......Justice Department Attorney and assistant to
Blackburn, 1979 trial. Assistant
United States Attorney, 1980 to the
present.

Victor Worheide, Esq.....Justice Department attorney for Grand Jury Hearings.

James Proctor............Chief Prosecutor 1970 to 1975. Judge Dupree's

        soninlaw.
Paul Stambaugh...........FBI   Forensics
    Lab 1979 trial and Grand Jury Hear-
    ings.
Peter Kearns.............Headed   the   CID
    Army reinvestigation.
William Ivory............CID   Investiga-
    tor, 1970
Franz Grebner............CID   Investiga-
    tor, 1970
Robert B. Shaw...........CID   Investiga-
    tor, 1970

        CONFESSORS TO THE CRIMES*

Helena Stoeckley, Greg Mitchell, Cathy
Perry.
(*Corroborated by over 30   new   witnesses
in addition to the original witnesses.)

THE DREYFUS CASE

In many ways, the Dreyfus case is strikingly similar to the MacDonald case. MacDonald was wrongfully accused and convicted of the murders of his family. Dreyfus was wrongfully accused and convicted of high treason. Both MacDonald and Dreyfus were officers in their respective armies when the crimes occurred. Scandals within the country's judicial system and shocking government cover-ups were at the core of both cases.

It was finally the outraged French public who came to Dreyfus' rescue. Their feelings were relayed to the French government and the French judicial system through Emile Zola's writings in a book titled, "J'accuse La Verite en Marche." Dreyfus was subsequently pardoned and absolved of the crimes.

In any large organization, there are the outstanding, the competent, the mediocre and the few who do not meet the organization's standards.

When certain individuals in our CID, FBI and Justice Department are criticized herein, the criticisms are aimed at the individuals, rather than at their respective organizations.

SCRUPLES

1

Alfred Dreyfus was a young husband,
a young father, a brilliant officer. Life
indeed seemed to reserve for him only
smiles.

During the Fall of 1894, Captain
Alfred Dreyfus was summoned to appear for
a routine inspection. Instead, he was
summarily accused of high treason. This
was the start of a twelve year fight for
freedom which included imprisonment on
Devil's Island, the discovery and cover-
up of numerous forgeries, accusations
against the French Army, the French
government and the French Judicial
system--and subsequently Dreyfus' pardon
on September 19, 1899, with his rank and
privileges restored on July 13, 1906.

Jeffrey MacDonald was a young
husband, a young father, a brilliant
doctor and an officer. Life indeed seemed
to reserve for him only smiles.

During the Winter of 1970, Captain
Jeffrey MacDonald was in the officer's

mess, about to sit down to dinner when a
news bulletin came over the public
address system, announcing that he,
Jeffrey MacDonald, was the chief suspect
in the brutal murders of his wife,
Colette, and two daughters, Kimberly and
Kristen. This was the start of a fight
for his freedom which has now reached its
sixteenth year and has included imprisonment at three Federal insti-
tutions: Terminal Island, California;
Bastrop, Texas, and Phoenix, Arizona,
where he is now. It has included the
discovery of government suppressed physical evidence which supports his innocence, new witnesses to the crimes, and
accusations against the U.S. Army's Criminal Investigation Division, (CID), The
United States Government, the United
States Department of Justice, and the
FBI.

At the present time, there is no end
in sight to MacDonald's unjust imprisonment, and his fate is as Dreyfus'
fate was--in the hands of the people who
dictate to our government the standards
of justice and constitutional rights they
are obligated to uphold.

At the core of the Dreyfus case, one
repeatedly encounters a major debate over
obedience, hierarchy and authority, which
often ignores, and in fact overrules,
justice. The same situation aptly describes the MacDonald case, where many,
out of traditional deference to the law
of the state, their own selfish convictions, or the ruses of ambition, find

compromises.

At the conclusion of the Army's Article 32 Hearing of the murders, which exonerated MacDonald, the presiding officer, Colonel Warren Rock, ordered the Army to investigate Helena Stoeckley. Stoeckley was a drug informant for the police and government agencies. MacDonald had described her as one of the assailants who had attacked his family and whom witnesses had seen in the area during the early morning hours of February 17, 1970, when the murders took place. The Army appointed CID agent Peter Kearns to head up a reinvestigation of the case. However, upon conferring with James Proctor, the chief prosecutor in the case at the time, Kearns all but defied Col. Rock's orders--perhaps to cover up the army's inept investigation of the crime scene and/or to protect Helena Stoeckley's informant status--and set his sights on proving MacDonald's guilt.

Following the reinvestigation, Proctor attempted to convince U.S. Attorney for the district of North Carolina, Warren H. Coolidge to indict MacDonald on virtually the same evidence which had exonerated him--but was refused by Coolidge, for lack of evidence.

The government would have been quite content, in fact, to bury the case forever, because Helena Stoeckley and her group were involved in a government operation far more serious than catching drug pushers.They were, according to Justice Department scuttlebutt, involved in procuring LSD for illegal "mind control" experiments being performed on soldiers returning to Fort Bragg from Vietnam, without their knowledge. One soldier, involved in an LSD mind control experiment, jumped out of a ninth floor window at Fort Bragg and died on impact with the earth--under which he was quickly and quietly buried.

The deaths of Colette, Kimberly and Kristen MacDonald would also have been quickly and quietly buried by the government had it not been for MacDonald's fanatical father-in-law, Alfred (Fred) Kassab. Kassab, from the time he met MacDonald as a young teenager, until over a year after the deaths of his step-daughter and grandchildren, was one of MacDonald's most loyal and staunch supporters. Then, quite suddenly and violently, Kassab turned on MacDonald and campaigned relentlessly against him until the Justice Department reluctantly appointed one of its lawyers, Victor Worheide, known for his reputation as a troubleshooter, to reopen the case.

The question, "Why did Kassab turn on MacDonald?" has been asked time and time again. It is surely not, as Kassab states, because of evidence of MacDonald's guilt found in the Article 32 Hearing transcripts--for they are the very transcripts which exonerated MacDonald. In over a thousand pages, there is literally nothing to tie MacDonald to the crimes.

Perhaps, however, the answer lies in

part with a statement Mildred Kassab's
sister Helen made in a letter to Mac-
Donald shortly after the murders. Here
she says:"...You are still ours. You are
perfect in every way and we love you so
much, we'll never let you go." True of
most of MacDonald's friends, is a deep
and unrelenting feeling of dependency on
him to dispense a sense of security,
leadership, devotion and well-being to
them...thereby creating an unparalleled
and charismatic sense of pleasure, which
is quite naturally habit-forming to all
but the most spirited.

As candid, open and giving as Mac-
Donald is concerning some aspects of himself and his life, he is religiously
closemouthed and uncompromising about
other aspects, particularly when they
relate to the reasoning and motivations
behind his decision-making processes.

MacDonald tends to make all who know
him feel that they are, if not the only
one, uniquely privileged, confided in and
loved. He is capable of extreme closeness, despite the fact that there is
always a distinct distance between himself and others. When this distance
closes in, MacDonald reacts, in retrospect, predictably to the situation, but
unpredictably, of course, to the person
who does not understand that he has,
though graciously invited, trespassed
into unwelcome territory. Perhaps this
is what happened to Kassab, who is not
the kind of person to take a rebuff
lightly. Both Fred and Mildred Kassab

wanted MacDonald close by and at their beck and call.

MacDonald, with the passing of time after the funerals, felt life closing in on him. He had been accused of the murders of his wife and two daughters, despite those he accused having been seen by witnesses going to and from his house --and massive forensic evidence of in- truders having been in his house. He had recuperated from a chest wound, which ac- cording to the doctors who testified at the Article 32 Hearing, came within a fraction of an inch of killing him. He had attended the funeral of his entire family. He was confined to quarters. He testified at the Article 32 Hearing for hours and days and then waited week after week after week until he was finally exonerated. Finally he was free. . . but was he?

Day in and day out, in-depth delib- erations with the Kassabs took place about the murders of his family. They asked him about every detail of every wound suffered by Colette, Kimberly and Kristen. Moreover, Kassab appeared to feel that it was MacDonald's personal obligation to track down those who murdered his family. MacDonald, on the other hand, felt compelled to pick up the pieces of his life and go forward, because with nothing besides Colette, Kimberly and Kristen on his mind, their memories became too painful for him to bear. As Dante once said: "There is no greater grief than to remember days of joy when misery is at hand." It has been said by many who had been close to both families that the Kassabs translated MacDonald's attitude as desertion. It is also quite possible that the Kassabs reacted to the news as a severe loss of emotional and financial security. This is perhaps logical because after the Article 32 Hearing, when MacDonald's sister Judy thanked the Kassabs for their support, Kassab told her not to give it a thought because Jeff was a doctor and would always support them in their time of need.

Upon hearing of MacDonald's plans to practice Emergency Medicine in California, the Kassabs told him that if he left them and abandoned their plans to find the murderers of his family, they would "get him." Though MacDonald did not take this threat seriously at the time and wrote the Kassabs compassionate, trusting letters through the early part of 1972, in retrospect, they had begun their vendetta almost simultaneously to MacDonald's touching California soil.

From that moment until now, as in the Dreyfus case, hierarchy and authority have ignored, and in fact overruled, justice. The Grand Jury proceedings were used as a prosecutorial tool rather than a presentation of all of the available evidence. The 1979 trial was an unsurpassed mockery of justice with crucial defense evidence withheld from the jury by a judge whose son-in-law had been one of MacDonald's chief prosecutors. The

same judge presided over MacDonald's
1984-85 Evidentiary Hearings and despite
over 30 new witnesses who corroborated
the confessions of three of the assailants MacDonald described, and newly
discovered physical evidence clearly supporting MacDonald's recollection of the
crimes, MacDonald was refused a new
trial.

On December 17, 1985, the Fourth
Circuit Court of Appeals supported this
judge's findings. The court's reaction to
the followiing letter, which I wrote,
illustrates their complete disregard for
upholding justice in the case of Jeffrey
MacDonald and makes one wonder just how
closely politics may be interwoven with
"justice."

January 8, 1986

The Honorable Harrison L. Winter
Chief Judge
4th Circuit Court of Appeals
U.S. Court House
10th and Main Streets
Richmond, Virginia 23219

Dear Judge Winter:

A telephone call on Friday, January 3 of
this year, from Peter Kearns, one of the
CID investigators in United States of
America versus Jeffrey R. MacDonald,
(case number 85-6208) prompted me to
write to you and ask for your advice.

Mr.Kearns, who has stated to me that he
has kept in close touch with Mr. Murtaugh
on this case, told me that he knew before
your December 17 decision in favor of the
government that:

1) the decision would be "3-zip."
2) there will be no rehearing en banc
   by your court.
3) the Supreme Court will refuse to
   hear the case.
4) the next time he and I meet will be
   on April 5, 1991, at a parole hearing for Dr. MacDonald.

Mr. Kearns' claim to this knowledge, as
you can well imagine, is extremely dis-
turbing to me; particularly combined with
the fact that certain points in the
decision contradict well-documented evidence to the contrary. Perhaps it is possible that something is going on in your
court of which you are not aware. On the
other hand, it may be that due to the
large volume of documents in the court
record of this case that certain of these
documents were lost in transit or overlooked. I bring several of the incorrect
statements in the decision to your attention, so that you will be better able to
understand my concerns and advise me
accordingly.

Decision: Page 3, II, paragraph 1.
'This evidence consists primarily of post
trial statements by Helena Stoeckley and
one each by two of her former associate

drug addicts.'

Contrary to this statement, there is evidence of over 30 witnesses in your court record who corroborate the confessors. Among them are a number of upstanding American citizens, who signed affidavits and are qualified not only to testify to a jury but to sit on a jury. The witnesses I speak of include:

1) The Reverend Phillips, a licensed minister.
2) Ann Sutton Canady, a counselor from the Reverend Phillips' ministry.
3) Juanita Sisneros, a counselor from the Reverend Phillips' ministry.
4) Blain O' Brien, a deputy sheriff.
5) John Humphries, a former MP and member of the Police Reserve.
6) James R. Nance, lawyer (of Betty Garcia).
7) Edith Boushey, a retired English Professor at North Carolina State University.
8) Carlos Torres, a retired sergeant.

Other witnesses who are citizens in good standing and have no history of drug or alcohol abuse include:
1) Frank Bushey
2) Addie Willis Johnstone
3) Joan Sonderson
4) Dorothy Averitt (who testified at the evidentiary hearing that she saw Stoeckley just hours after the murders and that Stoeckley smelled

"like a hog killing").
5) Bryant Lane
6) Norma Lane
7) Shirley J. Cole

Surely, since these witnesses corroborate the statements of the confessors and are qualified to sit on a jury, they are qualified to be heard by a jury.

Decision: Page 5, paragraph 2.
'The details she (Helena Stoeckley) gave contained many inconsistencies with MacDonald's version of what occurred and with the circumstantial evidence derived from the scene.'

-- Stoeckley said she carried a lighted candle and candle wax was found that was inconsistent with the candle wax from the candles owned by the MacDonald family.

-- Stoeckley said the spring in Kristen's hobby horse was broken. The prosecution said Stoeckley could have deduced it was broken from a newspaper picture. However, it is impossible, even with perfect vision, to deduce that it was broken, from the picture. Do you have this picture in your records?

-- A strand of brown hair was found in Colette MacDonald's hairbrush. Colette, Jeff, Kimberly and Kristen all had blond Hair. Helena Stoeckley had brown hair.

All of the above evidence is clearly documented and irrefutable.

Page 6.
'There is substantial doubt that these
hearsay statements would be admissible
since corroborating circumstances do not
clearly indicate their trustworthiness.'

In regard to "hearsay statements": How
can Stoeckley have been found to be reliable at trial and unreliable at the
1985 Evidentiary Hearings? How can Stoeckley on the one hand be counted upon by
police to act as one of their most
outstanding and reliable informants with
numerous arrests and convictions being
made on her testimony...yet be considered unreliable when it comes to her
testimony in the case of Jeffrey Mac-
Donald?
    Morally, logically and legally,
Stoeckley cannot be both. Since she has
been reliable time and time again for the
government, she must be considered reliable in the defense of Jeffrey Mac-
Donald.
    In regard to "corroborating cir-
cumstances": Helena Stoeckley says Greg
Mitchell killed Colette. Blood was found
on Colette MacDonald's hand and there is
a 50 percent chance that it was type O
blood. Greg Mitchell had type O blood.
Dr. Ronald K. Wright stated that Colette
MacDonald's wounds indicated that she had
been killed with blows consistent with a
left-handed swing. Greg Mitchell, according to a signed affidavit from his

wife, was left-handed. In addition, two reliable witnesses, Ann Sutton Cannady and Juanita Sisneros, identified Greg Mitchell as running from a farmhouse. Moments later, these witnesses saw the words "I killed MacDonald's wife and children" written in red paint still so fresh it was wet and dripping. Two more reliable witnesses, Norma and Bryant Lane, stated that Greg Mitchell told them of his fear of being apprehended for something bothering him, too horrible to even talk about, that happened at Ft. Bragg. He said he was afraid the FBI was after him and asked for money so that he could leave the country.

Decision: Page 6, paragraph 2.
'If these hearsay statements had been before the jury, it is most unlikely that the jury would have given them any credence.' Since numerous arrests and convictions were made on Helena Stoeckley's information; and because Dr. Rex Julian Beaber of The University of California at Los Angeles (his credentials are in the court record) stated in a signed affidavit that "when Helena Stoeckley confessed, she was fully competent and capable of perceiving, understanding, and remembering events," surely a jury has the right to consider Helena Stoeckley's confessions and the corroborating statements made by the many witnesses fully qualified to testify.

In addition, how can your court ignore

the thousands of citizens and numerous congressmen including Glenn Anderson, who has gone on record (press release chapter 9) with his thousands of constituents in stating that a new trial is mandated at the very least? The above citizens are "the man in the street," and according to our justice system their feelings should be considered in the name of law and the human rights to which we are all entitled.

Decision: Page 6, Paragraph 2.
'The circumstantial evidence made a strong case against MacDonald and demonstrated that his story was a fabrication entirely or in substantial part.'

When one considers that:

-- the pajama top demonstration presented to Dr.MacDonald's 1979 trial jury was a hoax because when the 48 holes were aligned with 21 wounds, many of those holes contradicted the directionality of the thrusts

-- The FBI's blood-typing results did not agree with the CID's blood-typing results according to Dr. Thomas Noguchi, Chairman, Board of Directors, National Association of Medical Examiners and Vice President of the World Association of Medical Law. (Dr. MacDonald's defense was not previously informed of the FBI's blood-typing results and is entitled to examine the FBI's blood-typing results as a matter of law.)

The 'strong' case against Dr. MacDonald weakens considerably.

Decision: Page 9, C, paragraphs 1 and 2. 'During an autopsy performed on the body of Mrs. MacDonald, scrapings were taken from under her fingernails and placed in a vial. An Army investigator reported that he saw in the vial what he believed to be a small piece of skin. Thereafter, detailed laboratory analysis was performed, and the report of the analysis contains no mention of any skin. Either the investigator was mistaken in believing that what he had seen in the vial was a small piece of skin, or the piece of skin was lost.'

There is no doubt that skin scrapings were taken from Colette MacDonald's fingernails and were lost or destroyed. The government, in fact, stated this in its brief. Even the district court stated that the doctor conducting Colette's autopsy noted in his report, "a small fragment of skin is found under the left little fingernail." In addition, records of the Army's crime laboratory showed that the skin fragment was subsequently sent to the lab. It was at the lab that the Army investigator saw the skin fragments and pointed them out to a chemist. The autopsy report and lab records are irrefutable proof that the skin was either lost or destroyed by the government.

Decision: Page 9, C, paragraph 3.
'Interestingly, there were scratches on
Dr. MacDonald's chest, which might have
been made by Mrs. MacDonald if her husband were her slayer.'

Why would a layman's description be
chosen by your court rather than the
expert medical testimony at trial that
there were only puncture wounds on Dr.
MacDonald's chest? Page 9 of the decision alone brings about serious question as to whether all the documents in
the record have been made available
and/or been reviewed by the judges considering the case.

Decision: Page 10, top paragraph.
'In a handwritten note, he stated that
the letter "g" seemed to resemble the "g"
in the word "Pig" that had been painted
on the headboard of the MacDonald's bed.
That word also had been fingerpainted,
but there was expert opinion that it had
been done by one wearing rubber gloves,
for there were no traces of ridges. Dr.
MacDonald had such gloves, of course, and
pieces of one were found on the bed near
the headboard and in a pile of bed-clo-
thing.'

Doctors "peel" off their rubber gloves
from top (the arm) to tip (the fingers)
in a split second or two. Only someone
inexperienced with rubber gloves (like a

drug-crazed hippie, for instance) would tear rubber gloves in the process of removing them. Do you not believe therefore, that it is inappropriate for the court to accuse Dr. MacDonald of wearing and tearing the gloves upon removal when this is not at all characteristic of something a doctor would do?

Page 10-11, E, Paragraph 1.
'The district judge concluded that the governnment had not deliberately suppressed anything and had acted in complete good faith.'

Whether you choose to believe that the government deliberately or not suppressed critical evidence supporting Dr. MacDonald's recollection of the crimes, the government, in the MacDonald case, does not have a history of acting in good faith. Brian Murtaugh was chastised by Judge Butzner on October 8, 1975, for withholding evidence from the defense; and Murtaugh recently broke the law for by-passing your court in order to revoke Dr. MacDonald's bail. Sam Currin was found to be lying under oath in another North Carolina case involving a woman who worked for Dr. MacDonald's attorney, Wade Smith. And then, of course, there's the FBI blood-typing...

The life of a man who has done much for his fellowman and his country is in your hands. I am in possession of copies of just about every "known" document on this

case. I have been in Judge Dupree's
courtroom and I have been in your
courtroom. I am an American citizen who
believes our system of justice must work,
and who will not, under any circumstance,
give up until Dr. MacDonald has received
the justice to which he is entitled.

As Chief Judge of the 4th Circuit Court,
I understand that it is your responsibility to correct the serious and
provable errors in the decision. I assume
you will do this because I am told that
you are an honorable man with a flawless
reputation.

As stated in the beginning of my letter,
I am in urgent need of your advice as to
what to do regarding the possibility
that, in view of Mr. Kearns conversation
with me, this case has been "fixed" from
"above."

I will be in the Richmond area the week
of January 20. Would it be possible for
me to meet with you and to take just a
small amount of your time to receive your
much needed help and advice on this
matter? Thank you for your consideration.

Sincerely,/Melinda Stephens

    The only reply to this letter was an
acknowledgement stating that it had been
received and placed on file. Warren
Burger, Chief Justice of the Supreme
Court at the time the Fourth Circuit

Court reviewed MacDonald's case, states
that, "A court which is final and unreviewable needs more careful scrutiny
than any other. Unreviewable power is the
most likely to self-indulge itself and
the least likely to engage in dis-
passionate self-analysis. In a country
like ours, no public institution, or the
people who operate it, can be above
public debate."

The Fourth Circuit Court does not,
apparently, share Chief Justice Burger's
views on this subject.

As in all governments, there are
those who strive to accomplish for the
good of their fellow man; and then there
are the small-minded, who care only for
themselves--who will lie, cheat, even
kill to preserve their image of success.
Both Alfred Dreyfus and Jeffrey MacDonald
became victims of the small-minded but
very powerful politicians of their
respective governments.

What similarities, many people ask,
did these two men have in common to
surive the horrors put upon them? Their
backgrounds are miles apart in many more
ways than distance and culture. Dreyfus
inherited from his peers a very narrow
view of the world. He never called into
question the order into which he was
placed nor the virtues he had been
taught. He contested nothing in the
society in which he lived and suffered.

MacDonald, on the other hand, loudly
decries the self-serving society who
blind themselves to his plight; and

deplores with a vengeance the actions of the government officials who have wrongfully convicted him to serve their own interests.

Like Dreyfus, MacDonald has a quasi-religious faith in the virtues of his country and in the victory of justice and truth. Some see this as a sign of naive obstinacy; yet if these two men did not possess such powerful certitude, it is doubtful they could survive the treatment to which they have been subjected.

Though Dreyfus came from wealth and MacDonald from a blue collar background, both were brought up to the commitments of honor, family and country.

MacDonald grew up in Patchogue, a small town on Long Island, in New York. His father was an electrical designer for the Brookhaven National Laboratory. His mother worked as a school nurse. Though MacDonald expresses fond memories of his childhood and was devoted to both parents, particularly his mother, from his early school years he began to strive for a better place in life. One of MacDonald's school teachers, Hedy Lonero, recalls his inquisitiveness, his disciplined study habits and a maturity beyond his years with respect to sensitivity and thoughtfulnness toward his fellow students.

When MacDonald attended Princeton, the librarian, who still keeps in touch with him, stated to me in a letter dated September 9, 1985, that "His control of

the situation all these years is a
measure of the strength of the man...and
for me, a never ending source of admiration. At its root has to be his
knowledge of the truth, and the grace of
providence supporting a good man. . .
amazing grace. With it man can surmount
any hardship. I pray every day that it
will always be with Jeffrey until it sees
him restored to his rightful place in
life."

When it comes to intellectual
pursuits, MacDonald has occasionally been
called arrogant. MacDonald has an
unquestionably brillliant mind and he
knows it. He is a perfectionist, notably
in the field of Emergency Medicine, where
he demands the highest standards from his
colleagues.

As one of the nation's foremost
emergency physicians, MacDonald helped
found both our country's paramedic and
trauma systems and consequently is responsible for saving countless lives including those of two Long Beach, California, policemen. Shortly before his
1979 conviction, MacDonald was given the
honor of being the first lifetime
honorary member of the Long Beach Police
Association. And it was the police who
organized a fundraiser to help pay the
cost of MacDonald's 1979 trial defense.

When MacDonald was convicted, however, his good deeds were quickly
forgotten by all but his closest friends,
medical colleagues and defense team. The
higher place in our society MacDonald

strived for and so successfully contributed to has all but deserted him. Not surprisingly, MacDonald is bitter. He is sad, lonely, afraid and confused; yet like Dreyfus, amid the worst suffering, he maintains a calm, cool and collected appearance to all but the few closest to him.

All in all, MacDonald is an exceptionally gentle person and is acutely atuned to the sensitivities of those with whom he comes into contact. He can be kind to the point of martyrdom, at which point his naivete and vulnerability are quickly and brutally taken advantage of by unscrupulous opportunists. These weaknesses have all too often caused those who are wise to the ways of the world to sadly state that MacDonald is his own worst enemy.

MacDonald is as disciplined and compulsive in some areas as he is impulsive in others. He is a stickler for accuracy in the documents concerning his case, and will go over and over them to make sure they are both correct and clearly stated. Yet he will decide whether or not to trust a member of the press, who can influence millions of people for or against him, in less than a minute. His impulsiveness has tended to be fully utilized by his foes and has often, but not always, given him cause for regret. Perhaps MacDonald's impulsiveness has been created and augmented through his many years of strife because his patience sometimes simply runs out.

MacDonald is meticulous and insistent upon cleanliness and order. The nurses who have worked with him over the years fondly recall his most frequent orders to them, which are to "keep the gurneys clean." MacDonald has, however, historically put human needs and feelings first, leaving dust and clutter aside to play with his daughters, whom he impulsively bought a pony for because he loved to see them happy.

On March 10, 1970, several weeks after the deaths of his family, MacDonald wrote a letter to Fred and Mildred Kassab. In the letter he said, "I love Colette more than anything in the world. I know she was happy as long as we were together and I will never be the same person without her. We had a beautiful family and although my family is gone, it helps me just a little to remember that Colette and Kim and Kristy and I had as much happiness in the short years together as most families have in a lifetime."

It is true, MacDonald has never again been the same person he was with Colette. He is afraid to love. He is afraid to trust. And he is afraid to be happy. MacDonald is not, however afraid to fight for the freedom he so dearly cherishes.

Most important of all, MacDonald, like Dreyfus, believes in the irresistible triumph of truth and his final proclamation of innocence with a force neither suffering nor his failures can breach. MacDonald survives as Dreyfus did, with a combination of fantastic courage and invincible convictions. . . which is not a bad definition of a hero.

I PLEDGE
ALLEGIANCE

2

Given the obligation to recall the
struggle waged by Dr.Jeffrey MacDonald on
behalf of his innocence and of justice
and truth, I must speak out about those
men who are so passionately bent on
destroying him--and who, feeling themselves doomed were he to be saved, continue to attack him with the desperate
daring of fear.

Can I silence their lies?

Can I silence their crimes?

If so, I would be silencing his
virtue.

Can I silence the outrage and the
slander with which they pursue him?

If so, I would be silencing his due
compensation and his honor.

Can I silence their shame?

If so, I would be silencing his
glory.

Let us envy him. He has honored his
country and the world with his immense
body of work and good deeds.

Let us envy him. His destiny and his courage have combined to endow him with the greatest of fates.

He is a moment in the conscience of humanity.

I ACCUSE

3

PROLOGUE

Is the reputation of the U.S. Army, the U.S. Department of Justice, the FBI and the U.S. Government, more important to protect than the life of one innocent American citizen?

Is it more important to protect the government informants who killed Mac-Donald's wife, two daughters and unborn son in order to cover up the true story behind the LSD experiments these informants helped to provide drugs for at Fort Bragg?

Is the confidence of the American people in our Army, judges, the FBI and our government more important than upholding the constitution of our Country? And is there a double standard where liberty and justice for all are concerned?

Do we have two systems of values in this country, as there were in France when Dreyfus was convicted of high treason?

> "I am convinced of Dreyfus' inno-
> cence," a French officer stated,
> "but if his verdict were up to me,
> I would convict him for the honor
> of the Army."

In sacrificing MacDonald to protect
government informants and the law brea-
kers in our Army, FBI, and Justice Department, do we save the honor of our
Country, or do we encourage the kind of
rampant injustice our forefathers fought
so hard to protect us against?

If you believe in the honor of the
whole, no matter what the consequences to
the rights of the individual, then you
are indeed satisfied that Jeffrey Mac-
Donald has been rightfully imprisoned.

If you believe in the rights of the
individual, however, then is it not your
duty to join the fight for liberty and
justice for Dr. Jeffrey MacDonald?

I ACCUSE

CID investigators Grebner, Shaw and
Ivory of negligence and prejudice against
Jeffrey MacDonald for:

A) Failing to acknowledge and establish
   the presence of intruders in the
   MacDonald home despite 45 known items
   which indicate the presence of
   intruders. The 45 items include, but
   are not limited to:

a. Candlewax, that according to a CID lab report was not from the MacDonald residence and was found on the bedspread and a chair in one of the bedrooms and on the coffee table in the living room.
b. Three weapons, used in the commission of the crimes, that did not come from the MacDonald home.
c. A jewelry box, containing reddish brown stains and one latent unidentified fingerprint and one latent unidentified palm print.
d. Eight jewelry items, missing from the jewelry box. Claims for these items were approved for payment by the CID per the CID document on pages 51-53. These items were described as: one heart-shaped diamond ring, one star sapphire ring, one class ring, one silver I.D. bracelet, one 24K gold wedding band, one black onyx ring, one antique gold railroad watch and one 24K gold watch chain.
e. One strand of brown hair found in Colette's hand and not identified as belonging to anyone in the MacDonald family, all of whom had blond hair.
f. 11 unidentified fingerprints (not including the one found on the jewelry box).
g. 16 unidentified palmprints (not including the one found on the jewelry box).

h. One bloody syringe
i. One broken back door lock.

B) Neglecting to submit 29 unidentified finger and palmprints to the FBI, thereby failing to attempt to locate the bearers of these finger and palmprints, whose identities could have proven the crimes were committed by the assailants MacDonald described and thereby exonerated MacDonald.

Kimberly MacDonald's Bedroom

a. One unidentified fingerprint located 4'-3-1/2" from floor and 4'-3/4" from doorknob to the center of mass of the print.
b. Two unidentified palmprints located 4'-5-1/2" from floor and 5'-3/4" from the hall side into the jamb.
c. One unidentified fingerprint 3' 9-1/2" from floor and 1/2" from the wall side into the jamb.

Colette and Jeff MacDonald's Bedroom

a. One fingerprint and one palmprint, both unidentified, located 4' 8-1/4" from floor on door jamb inside bedroom near light switch.
b. One unidentified fingerprint located 4'-7" from floor on door jamb inside bedroom near light switch.
c. One unidentified palmprint located 5'1-1/2" from floor, on inside of

jamb measured from print master bedroom side toward hall 5".

d. One unidentified palmprint located 4'10" from floor, on jamb measured from print master bedroom side toward hall 5".

e. One unidentified palmprint located 3' 6-1/2" from floor, on jamb measured from print master bedroom side toward hall 6-1/4".

f. One unidentified palmprint located 3' 4-1/2" from floor, measured from print toward hall 6-1/4".

g. Two unidentified fingerprints located 4' 11" from floor on hall side of jamb by light switch.

h. One unidentified fingerprint located 4' 6" from the floor on inside of jamb nearest north wall.

Utility Room

a. One unidentified palm print located 4' 3" from floor on cast jamb on inside south wall of utility room.

b. One identified palmprint located 5' 3" from floor on east jamb on inside south wall of utility room.

c. One unidentified print (lost).

d. Bureau: One identified palmprint located on southeast corner of bureau next to utility room door.

Bath-Hall Closet

a. One unidentified palmprint located 5' 3" from floor, southside of

bathroom door jamb nearest hall closet.
b. One unidentified fingerprint located 5' 1-1/2" from floor, south-side of bathroom door jamb nearest closet.

Kristen MacDonald's Bedroom

a. One unidentified palmprint located 4' 6-1/4" from floor, inside door-jamb on west side.
b. One unidentified fingerprint in hall on west door jamb 4' 5" from floor.
c. Two unidentified palmprints inside door jamb on east side 4' 10" from floor.
d. One unidentified fingerprint inside door jamb on west side 4' 6-3/4" from floor.
e. One unidentified palmprint inside doorjamb on west side 4' 5" from floor.
f. One unidentified fingerprint inside door jamb on west side 4' 2" from floor.

Kitchen

a. One unidentified fingerprint top left drawer of sink cabinet 2'-6-1/2" from floor and 6" from south wall.

Venetian Blinds

    a. One unidentified fingerprint on edge of blind.

C) Failing to dust areas of the couch in the living room where MacDonald stated he was attacked, as well as other critical areas of the house, for finger and palmprints.

D) Falsely accusing MacDonald of staging the crime scene because there were not sufficient signs of a struggle nor evidence of intruders in the MacDonald home, despite:

    a. 45 items of evidence, including 29 unidentified finger and palmprints.
    b. A chest injury to MacDonald, which is unlikely a doctor would self inflict because, as numerous doctors testified, the injury was in an area where penetration could not be controlled and was capable of killing MacDonald.
    c. Injuries that match holes in MacDonald's pajama top which would be impossible to self inflict due to the direction of the thrusts.
    d. Claims for loss and damages incurred during the murders for 38 items confirmed by the following CID report.

DEPARTMENT OF THE ARMY
U. S. ARMY CLAIMS SERVICE
OFFICE OF THE JUDGE ADVOCATE GENERAL
FORT HOLABIRD, MARYLAND 21219

7 January 1971
JAGD-71-02-06-0037

Captain Jeffrey R. MacDonald
68 Mount Vernon, Apt. 1-E
Patchogue, New York, 11772

Dear Captain MacDonald:

Your claim, for loss and damage to your household goods, arising out of the events of the night of 16-17 February,1970, at your assigned quarters at 544 Castle Drive, Fort Bragg, North Carolina, has been approved for payment in the amount of $3,171.75 under the provisions of Chapter 11, AR 27-20, implementing title 31, United States Code, sections 240-243, and has been certified to a disbursing officer for issuance of a check in that amount.

Based on the available evidence, we have concluded that the following items are either missing, damaged, or not being returned to you and are therefore compensable. References are to the line item numbers shown on the submitted forms 1089-1.

Item No.
7   Gold carpet 9'x12'

9   Rocker with orange and black cushion
10   Wooden Danish coffee table.
12   Wood frame Danish couch with cushions
13   Handmade multi-colored afghan
19   Large ceramic ash tray
20   Three ceramic frogs
76   Box, Valentine candy
99   Assorted packaged food (some were returned so the award for this item was estimated)
102 Assorted cleaning equipment
106 Bulletin board
124 Set bunk beds with double plaid mattresses (one returned, one approved for payment)
129 Two white bookcases (one returned, one approved for payment)
131 Three purple rugs
132 Pair of ceramic owls (one returned, one approved for payment)
136 Double bed
141 Two framed pictures of clowns (one returned, one approved for payment)
150 Heart-shaped diamond ring
151 Star sapphire ring
160 Class ring (1961)
162 Man's silver ID bracelet
163 Ladies' 24K wedding band
167 Man's ring, black onyx
168 Antique gold railroad watch
169 Watch chain, 24K gold
175 Pair wooden table lamps
176 Two bedside lamps
178 Double bed with mattress
179 Large chest of drawers
180 Two chests of drawers (3-drawer)

181 Mirror for double bureau
183 White wool pile rug
184 Green and purple throw rug
208 Pink rug
209 Blue wicker basket
210 Black and chrome stepladder

E) Failure to secure the crime scene.

   a. Dozens of M.P.'s, other Army per-
      sonnel and at least one neighbor,
      walked freely about the house mov-
      ing evidentiary items, and tracking
      dirt, grass, blood and fibers
      throughout, making it impossible to
      relate the position of the bodies
      and the rooms they were found in to
      their respective blood types, and
      to pinpoint the origin of the
      fibers from Dr. MacDonald's pajama
      top and bottom.
   b. Numerous articles including jewelry
      and Jeffrey MacDonald's wallet were
      stolen from the house. (MacDonald's
      wallet was recovered after having
      been taken by an ambulance driver.)
      In addition, potential exculpatory
      evidence is highly likely to have
      disappeared.

F) Failure to set up roadblocks to
   attempt to apprehend the four assailants MacDonald had described to
   the M.P.'s after being revived by
   mouth-to-mouth resuscitation.

G) Failure to comply with Fayetteville

police officer Beasley's radio call stating that he had apprehended the woman MacDonald described and was requesting back-up.

I accuse the Womack Hospital Administration of criminal negligence.

A)   Failure to preserve MacDonald's pajama bottoms which contained evidence supporting MacDonald's recollection of the crimes. (They were discarded.) The pajama bottoms were ripped from crotch to knee according to a hospital technician, who finally came forth five years after the trial. The rip in the pajama bottoms explained the presence of fibers in various rooms after MacDonald claimed he had taken off his pajama top.

I accuse CID investigator William Ivory of losing or purposely hiding or destroying a piece of skin found under Colette MacDonald's fingernail, which could have belonged to one of the intruders MacDonald described in artist conceptions and could have proven MacDonald's innocence beyond a reasonable doubt. Ivory was the last person in the chain of evidence to possess the piece of skin.
I accuse William Ivory of falsely stating that the pajama top MacDonald placed over his wife's chest had not been removed prior to being photographed. This statement is false because before

the photographers arrived, Ivory stated
that he had carefully examined Colette
MacDonald's chest for signs of respir-
ation and active bleeding. In order to
accomplish this, he would have had to
remove the pajama top to examine her
chest. Thus, the pajama top theory based
on MacDonald's placement of his top on
Colette is false to begin with because
they were working on the basis of Ivory's
placement of the pajama top on Colette,
rather than MacDonald's.

I accuse William Ivory of improperly storing the pajama top by
stuffing it into a plastic bag so that
blood seeped through layers of fabric
making it impossible to compare blood
types with their position of origin.

I accuse FBI scientist Paul Stombaugh of accepting the pajama top for
analysis despite an FBI policy which for-
bids analysis of improperly preserved
evidence.

I accuse Paul Stombaugh of presenting
MacDonald's trial jury with a theory he
knew was false. This theory stated that
MacDonald had stabbed his wife 48 times
through his pajama top. Stombaugh had
examined the holes in the pajama top in
preparation for his testimony to the
Grand Jury, approximately four years before the trial, and had stated that each
puncture indicated whether the hole was
made from the outside-in or from the

inside-out.

Yet when one of Stombaugh's technicians, Helen Green, was told to fold the garment to achieve forty-eight holes with Colette's twenty-one chest wounds, many of those holes contradicted the directionality of the thrusts, which totally disproves the basis for the theory and proves that Colette's wounds did not match the holes in MacDonald's pajama top. In addition, it substantiates MacDonald's claim of being attacked by drug-crazed hippies who, according to MacDonald's medical report, left him with numerous puncture wounds.

If you match certain of the holes in the pajama top to the wounds in MacDonald's chest and upper abdomen, they fit perfectly. Moreover, the location of the inside-out thrusts of the holes matched with their respective wounds, make self-infliction of these wounds an impossibility.

The location of other holes in the pajama top substantiates MacDonald's statement that in trying to remove his pajama top, it got caught up around his wrists, forcing him to use his wrists as a shield to fend off the intruders.

I accuse Paul Stombaugh of presenting Dr. MacDonald's trial jury with a theory of how MacDonald killed each member of his family based on the types of blood found in each room, knowing full well that:

A) Blood had been tracked through the house by dozens of people entering the unsecured crime scene, making it impossible to relate the position of the bodies and the rooms they were in to their respective blood types.

B) Considering the amount of blood evident in the killings, it is entirely logical that some of the blood contaminated the clothing of the assailants and was subsequently transferred by them from room to room. (This observation was made by Col. Rock at the Army's Article 32 Hearing.)

C) The CID blood typing which his theory was based on differed from the FBI's blood typing.

I accuse Paul Stombaugh of covering up the fact that the Army's bloodstain typing differed from the FBI's blood stain typing, so that MacDonald's defense could not fully dispute the basis of his theory. 2*

I accuse the CID of allowing MacDonald's step-father-in-law, Fred Kassab, access into the MacDonald home to examine the crime scene, during which time he mishandled critical evidence.

2 Thomas T. Noguchi, M.D. "Coroner at Large," page 84.
* Forensic's expert Dr. John Thornton

states: "There's a person I know who was
working at the Army Crime Lab in 1970, at
the time of the murders, when those blood
stains were typed. (Rowe, Professor, George Washington University, Washington
D.C.) He told me that in 1970 the FBI
had looked at the Army's blood typing and
found it was different from the FBI's own
blood typing."

I accuse Justice Department lawyer
Victor Worheide of purposely and mal-
iciously keeping testimony on behalf of
Dr. MacDonald's defense from the Grand
Jury.

A) Though Worheide stated that all
   suspects in the murders of Dr.
   MacDonald's wife and children were to
   testify before the Grand Jury, only
   MacDonald was called testify.
   At the conclusion of the Article 32
Hearing which exonerated MacDonald, the
presiding officer Col. Rock ordered "that
appropriate civilian authorities be
requested to investigete the alibi of
Helena Stoeckley, Fayetteville, North
Carolina, reference her activities and
whereabouts during the early morning
hours of 17 February 1970, based on
evidence presented at this hearing."
Neither Helena Stoeckley nor the other
three assailants MacDonald had described
were asked to testify before the Grand
Jury.

B) The Grand Jury had requested that Dr.

MacDonald undergo a sodium amytal (truth serum) test with the hope that the results would guide them in deciding whether or not he was telling the truth.

Though MacDonald agreed to take the test on February 1,1975, Worheide kept this fact from the Grand Jury and pressed them for and received an indictment before the test could take place and results given to the Grand Jury.

I accuse Victor Worheide of misusing the Grand Jury as a prosecutorial tool rather then the investigative tool it was created to be.

A) FBI and CID laboratory technicians were asked to testify to the Grand Jury. They presented their "Pajama Top," "Fiber," and "Blood" theories to the Grand Jury without ever allowing the Grand Jury to hear the Article 32 Hearing defense testimony on these subjects, which had exonerated MacDonald of the crimes.

> "The prosecutor should disclose to the Grand Jury any evidence which he knows will tend to negate guilt."
> -- The American Bar Association

I accuse James Blackburn, Assistant United States Attorney, and Brian Murtaugh, Justice Department Attorney at the time of MacDonald's 1979 trial, of allowing FBI forensics specialist Paul Stombaugh to present a theory pointing to MacDonald's guilt based on the types of blood found in each room, despite the fact that he was clearly aware of the blatant defects which formed the basis for this theory.

I accuse Blackburn and Murtaugh of breaking the Federal Rules of Criminal Procedure by refusing MacDonald's defense the government's 13-volume report on the case.

A) The 13-volume government report on the case, recently obtained by Maconald through FOIA, strongly implicated Greg Mitchell, one of the assailants MacDonald described, and the assailant Helena Stoeckley specifically stated killed Colette.1.

B) This report also led to many new witnesses, some of whom the prosecution had not informed the defense about at the time of the trial.

C) In addition, the report contained new forensic evidence which could have reversed the jury's verdict. 2

----

1. Greg Mitchell had type O blood—the type which was found on Colette's hand.
2. Greg Mitchell was left-handed, and according to Dr. Ronald K. Wright, Chief Medical Examiner, Broward County, Florida, the blow that killed Colette is consistent with a swing from a lefthanded

person.

I accuse Blackburn and Murtaugh of breaking the Federal Rules of Evidence by refusing to give the defense addresses of witnesses they required in preparation for the 1979 trial. (The defense finally obtained the witness information they required after a ruling in the defense's favor from the Fourth Circuit Court of Appeals.)

I accuse Blackburn and Murtaugh of refusing to allow defense forensic expert Dr. John Thornton adequate access to the MacDonald home in order to study the layout and relate the physical evidence to it.

I accuse Blackburn and Murtaugh of holding ex parte meetings and attempting to cover up these meetings, with MacDonald's 1979 trial judge, Franklin T. Dupree; and of collaborating with Judge Dupree against MacDonald in regard to withholding evidence from the defense and disallowing critical defense testimony to be presented to the jury.

I accuse Blackburn and Murtaugh of collaborating with "Fatal Vision" author Joe McGinniss to present false statements about the evidence in an attempt to convince the public of MacDonald's guilt.

1 See Chapter VI

I accuse Blackburn and Murtaugh of giving "Fatal Vision" producer Michael Rosenfeld, either personally or through McGinniss or an appointed agent, Freedom of Information Act (FOIA) material not at the time given to MacDonald, with the purpose of twisting evidence which actually supported MacDonald, and without MacDonald's permission, which is required by law.

I accuse Judge Franklin T. Dupree of refusing MacDonald's defense discovery and of personal prejudice against Mac-Donald.

A) March 23, 1979, marked the 5th (in a total of 29) letters to the government asking for the defense's right under the Federal Rule of Criminal Procedure 16 to have defense experts conduct a scientific examination of the evidence. Due to the government's refusal to make this evidence available for examination, a motion to compel the government to produce the physical evidence was filed on April 23, 1979. A motion for an expedited hearing on that issue was also filed. The court refused to grant an immediate hearing even though the motion was accompanied by an affidavit by Dr. John Thornton, a forensic science expert, stating that forensic science expert, stating that defense testing would require eight weeks from the date of receipt of the evidence.

Even though Judge Dupree had not seen or read the motion, the supporting affidavits and the memorandum of law, and although Judge Dupree had not read any of the cases cited in the memorandum which supported the defense's right to examine the physical evidence, and the government had not filed any opposing legal memoranda in the case, Judge Dupree pre-judged the motion, orally stating that he would not permit defense expert, Dr. Thornton, to examine the evidence in the laboratory he had chosen in California.

The court did not set a hearing on the motion until May 10, 1979. On May 18, 1979, Judge Dupree issued an oral order denying any part of the motion to have the evidence examined by Dr. Thornton in San Francisco, where both he and MacDonald's defense lawyer were located.

The end result was that while the government proceeded to trial with over nine years' opportunity to test, analyze and evaluate its evidence, the defense was given bits and pieces of evidence in North Carolina, where the murders and the trial took place, only days before the trial, with insufficient time and facilities to examine the evidence.

B) Judge Dupree refused to force the government to provide the defense with a list of addresses for witnesses the defense needed to contact pre-trial, making it necessary to go to the 4th Circuit Court, where Judge Butzner ruled in favor of giving the defense timely access to this information.

C) Judge Dupree refused to order the government to turn over its 13-volume report of the case, despite the fact that the Federal Rules of Criminal Procedure dictated that he do so. Had this 13-volume report been made available to the defense pre-trial, rather than post-trial through the Freedom of Information Act (FOIA), the jury would have heard the documented facts supporting Dr. MacDonald's recollection of the physical evidence, in addition to the blood type evidence, which in itself destroys the government's first degree murder theory.

  I accuse Judge Dupree of pre-judging (and without justification) motions to dismiss the case for denial of a speedy trial and of personal prejudice against MacDonald.

A) Judge Dupree entered an order denying MacDonald's motion to dismiss the

indictment due to denial of a speedy
trial, even though the record to present evidence was still open. The
defense had formally moved that Judge Dupree permit the defendant to
subpoena three officials of the Department of Justice.

These officials had personal knowledge of the circumstances of the
nearly five years' delay from when
MacDonald was first charged until his
indictment and arraignment. Even
though the testimony of these people
was essential for MacDonald to meet
his burden of proof, Judge Dupree did
not rule on these motions, leaving
the record open on them. He then
denied the motion to dismiss the
indictment for denial of a speedy
trial.
    Dr. Thomas Noguchi states, in his
book, "Coroner at Large": "The Army
hearing was, in effect, a real trial,
lasting for four months, with witnesses
examined and cross-examined on the stand
under rules of evidence. Unlike the trial
nine years later, it took place when the
events were fresh in the memories of the
witnesses, and all those witnesses were
available to testify."

    I accuse Judge Dupree of denying the
defense a change of venue without
consulting MacDonald's lawyer, and of
personal prejudice against MacDonald.

A) In seeking to find a basis upon which
to deny MacDonald a change of venue,
Judge Dupree called his friend, Judge
Ivory Hill, U.S. District Court of
the Central District of California,
to discuss the issue with him. This
call was made without prior knowledge
or approval of MacDonald and his
counsel. The conversation was not
transcribed and made available. No
opportunity was afforded the defense
to contest the opinions or challenge
the information that Judge Dupree
received from Judge Hill.

I accuse Judge Dupree of requesting
use by the court (allegedly an unbiased
instrument of justice) of Dr. Page Hudson, a government consultant, despite the
actual and potential conflict of interest
involved, and despite reminders of this
conflict of interest from Dr. Hudson. In
addition, Judge Dupree did not disclose
this knowledge to the defense...blatant
evidence of Judge Dupree's personal
prejudice against MacDonald.

I accuse Judge Dupree of holding ex
parte meetings with government prosecutors to discuss the handling of the
case and attempting to cover up this
fact--still another example of Judge Dupree's fanatical personal prejudice against MacDonald.

A) On a number of occasions since the

proceedings of the case began,   Judge
Dupree held ex parte conferences   in
his chambers with attorneys   for   the
government   concerning   legal   issues
that were raised by defense   counsel,
and were pending before the court   at
the time.

These matters included strategic   decisions the goverment had to make   in
connection with   the   prosecution   of
MacDonald. At no time did either   the
court or government counsel   disclose
to defense counsel   in   advance   that
such meetings were   to   be   held;   nor
did   they   make   any   disclosure   to
defense counsel after   the   meetings.
When all was   said   and   done,   Judge
Dupree had ruled against all   of   the
defense's 24   pre-trial   and   trial
motions and ruled for   seven   out   of
eight of the prosecution's   pre-trial
and trial motions.

    I accuse Judge Dupree of breaking an
agreement with the defense not to   use   a
psychiatric report from Drs. Brussell and
Silverman   who   had,   unknown   to   the
defense,   previously acted   as   government
agents in the case...and, in this matter,
I again accuse Judge   Dupree   of   blatant
personal prejudice against MacDonald.

A) Despite the fact that the   government
   had a psychiatric report on MacDonald
   from Walter Reed Army Hospital, Judge
   Dupree allowed psychiatrists, who   he

government early on in the case, to prepare another psychiatric report on MacDonald. Unlike the positive psychiatric report from Walter Reed Army Hospital, the Brussell-Silverman Report was predictably negative.

In an agreement dated August 13, 1979, it is stated "that if the court rules that the defendant Jeffrey R. MacDonald may not offer psychiatric evidence in support of his defense, that no part of any interview, test or evaluation made by either of you (Drs. Brussell and Silverman) may be disclosed to any person whatsoever except upon the written consent of Dr. MacDonald."

Despite this agreement, Judge Dupree used the report as grounds for denying Dr. MacDonald bail while his case was on appeal after the 1979 trial. (MacDonald was subsequently granted bail by the 4th Circuit Court of Appeals.)

I accuse Judge Dupree of tampering with jury selection due to his prejudice against prospective black jury members.

A) Judge Dupree told all the prospective black jurors except one (the token) to go home and "help their daddies pick the tobacco."

B) Judge Dupree endeared himself to the jury by complimenting them and sympathizing with all of them and then making his disdain for the defense obvious by expressions of boredom, impatience and distaste.

I accuse Judge Dupree of refusing to recuse himself from the case because his son-in-law was one of MacDonald's chief prosecutors, and this clearly constitutes an unlawful conflict of interest.

A) The former son-in-law of Judge Dupree, James Proctor, made public statements during the evidentiary hearings in a hometown newspaper where both he and the judge reside. The statements strongly urged that MacDonald's conviction stand, and included information about Proctor's getting an indictment and conviction in the case.

When a judge's impartiality has been questioned, the procedure is that he may not himself decide the merits of a motion to recuse himself. If he does decide the motion, (which he did), it is widely recognized that he has exceeded his jurisdiction. Federal statutes 28 U.S.C., 144 and 455 are statutory examples of this rule:

> "...extraordinary injustice can provoke extraordinary acts of concealment. Where such concealment is alleged, it ill behooves the government of a free people

the government of a free people
to evade an honest accounting."
--Judge J. Skelly Wright, U.S.
Court of Appeals

All of the accused here are Mac-
Donald's prosecutors. Their impulses toward omnipotence are means of fending off
anxiety and doubt, which stem from
negligence, incompetence and prejudice.
The pleasure they take in causing Mac-
Donald pain is a symptom of their omni-
potent ideologies.

Their motivations and behavior
combine psychological traits which exist
in many of us and, in their case, emerged
because of the psychological and moral
conditions of their environment. Crucial
to this emergence is an ideology or view,
a theory or vision which justifies or
demands evil action.

MacDonald's prosecutors, viewed in
this light, are similar in personality to
Dreyfus' prosecutors: emerging as vis-
ionary ideologues, efficiently perse-
cution--oriented functionalists, diligent
careerists--and disturbingly human.

EVIDENCE THE
JURY NEVER HEARD

4

PROLOGUE

For political gain, to cover up wrongdoing, weak men make heroes victims and let the guilty go free.

Dreyfus was accused by the Army of stealing documents from the German embassy in France. The German embassy says: "Here we can but repeat still again and forever that Dreyfus was and is absolutely unknown to our embassy, that we have never had any relations...be they direct or through an intermediary...with him, and that consequently, there has never existed in the embassy the alleged document written by him and stolen from the embassy, which is said to have led to his conviction. If Dreyfus' conviction did indeed result from an alleged document emanating from him and stolen from the German embassy, that conviction is in error, and after the declaration by the German ambassador to the minister of foreign affairs that the embassy never had the slightest dealings with Dreyfus, the French government should alone assume the weighty responsibility of this act of judicial murder."

MacDonald was accused by the Army of murdering his family. The people MacDonald described and accused of the crimes all existed, all knew each other and all had a motive to kill...drugs. The Army had a motive for covering up their crimes; a motive stemming from the fact that they were government informants involved in illegal LSD experiments at Ft. Bragg.

The agencies of the U.S. Government involved should alone assume the weighty responsibility for this act of judicial murder.

EVIDENCE THE JURY NEVER HEARD

On February 17, 1970, the Military Police found Jeffrey MacDonald unconscious, lying over his wife's body. When revived, MacDonald told the MP's that at least four people, including a black male in an Army jacket, two white men, and a blonde woman with a floppy hat, had attacked his family.

Despite witnesses who saw the people MacDonald described in the area after the murders, Army investigators charged MacDonald with the crimes, undoubtedly to protect their own informants and prevent the public from hearing about the illegal LSD experiments for which the informants provided drugs at Fort Bragg. The judicial branch of the Army provided a stumbling block, however.

At the conclusion of a five-month Army investigation, the charges against MacDonald were found to be "not true." As previously mentioned, Colonel Rock, who conducted the Army's Article 32 Hearings, ordered the CID to reinvestigate others, including Helena Stoeckley, who were identified through descriptions given by MacDonald and other crime scene witnesses.

A report written by FBI agent Mahon (working in cooperation with the CID) on April 30, 1971, gives a clue as to the depth of the investigation. Mahon states that, "Stoeckley was busy all day setting up narcotic buys for the police. She is providing them with real good information and this is the reason that the Nashville Police are reluctant to press her on the MacDonald issue at this time." Later in the report, Mahon says, "I know he (Lt. Bowlin of the Nashville Police Department) isn't going to break up a good thing as long as she is playing the role of the good informant...and she is providing outstanding information. I don't blame him."

In June of 1971 the CID "completed" its re-investigation, which stated that they were correct in their initial charges.

At the insistence of MacDonald's father-in-law, the CID "conclusions" were then passed around the U.S. Justice Department for years, with numerous lawyers, one after the other, refusing to prosecute.

During August, 1974, a former Army investigator in the CID re-investigation, Brian Murtaugh, who had become a civilian lawyer with the Justice Department after his discharge from the Army, decided to reopen the case by arranging for a Grand Jury in Raleigh, North Carolina. The Grand Jury met for six months, until January 1975, at which time they indicted MacDonald.

MacDonald was subsequently arrested by the FBI, jailed, and granted bail a week later.

In January of 1976 the 4th Circuit Court of Appeals overturned the indictment on "Speedy Trial" grounds and all charges were dismissed.

In May, 1978, the U.S. Supreme Court reversed the 4th's Circuit's ruling and ordered MacDonald to stand trial on the premise that one cannot prevent a trial by claiming speedy trial violations.

MacDonald's trial took place in August of 1979. MacDonald's defense was based on Helena Stoeckley's confession to the murders and seven witnesses who corroborated her presence at the scene of the crime. Judge Dupree refused to allow these seven witnesses to testify for the Defense. Their testimony would have included the following:

Officer P. E. Beasley...states that the day after the crimes he questioned Stoeckley about the MacDonald murders because she matched MacDonald's descr-

iption of one of the intruders. Stoeckley told Beasley, "In my mind, it seems
that I saw this thing happen," further
adding that she had been, "heavy on
mescaline." Beasley also asked Stoeckley about funeral wreaths which were
found hanging in her yard. Stoeckley, who
was dressed in black, responded that she
was mourning the MacDonalds.

William Posey...one of Stoeckley's
neighbors, testified that a few days
after the MacDonald slayings, Stoeckley
told him that although she did not kill
anyone herself, she held a light while
the crime was in progress. She said she
observed a "hobby horse thing," which was
broken in the apartment. She also told
Posey that she believed she had been seen
by a policeman on Honeycutt Street on
the morning of the crimes.

Jane Zillioux...a woman who befriended Stoeckley when Stoeckley moved
to Nashville shortly after the MacDonald
murders, testified that Stoeckley told
her that she could not return to Fayetteville (her former home near Mac-
Donald's) because she had been involved
in murders there of a woman and two small
children. She told Zillioux that she had
worn her white boots and blonde wig on
the night of the crimes, and that she was
in the company of three males the night
of the crimes, and "was with them for the
drugs." She described the murder scene
to Zillioux stating: "So much blood. I
couldn't see or think of anything except
blood..." She asked Zillioux not to re-

peat what had been said.

Charles Underhill...another friend of Stoeckley's in Nashville, testified that Stoeckley told him, while she was in a state of emotional distress: "They killed her and the two children...They killed the two children and her."

James Gaddis...a Nashville police officer to whom Stoeckley was providing information concerning drug traffic, testified that Stoeckley confided to him that she had been at the scene of the MacDonald murders and knew who was involved. She said that one of the participants drove a blue Ford Mustang.

Robert A. Brisentine...an Army investigator, testified that he interviewed Stoeckley in April of 1971. Stoeckley confessed that she had been present during the MacDonald murders but that she had not actively participated. She also offered to reveal the names of the participants and the circumstances surrounding the killings if granted immunity from prosecution. Subsequently, after telling Brisentine that it rained hard right after the murders, Stoeckley said, "I have already said too much," and recanted her statements. Brisentine also recalled that, "she knew about the blood on the bed." Further, at one point during the interview, Stoeckley told Brisentine that, "The hippie element was angry with Captain MacDonald as he would not treat them by prescribing methadone for their addiction to drugs."

Wendy Rouder...one of MacDonald's

trial counsel, testified that she visited Stoeckley in the wake of a report that Stoeckley had been assaulted shortly after she had testified. Rouder testified that during the course of their conversation, Stoeckley acknowledged that she had "a memory of standing on the couch (in the MacDonald home), holding a candle...." Asked whether she had ever lost her sense of guilt concerning the murders, she replied, "No, what do you think I have taken all these damn drugs for?" Asked why she would not state her recollections in court, Stoeckley replied, "I can't, with those damn prosecutors standing there."

According to the study, Stoeckley's statements indicated an intimate knowledge of the murder scene. She remembered having seen a "hobby horse thing" and blood on the bed, both found at the scene. Consistent with MacDonald's account, she stated that she had held a candle during the murders, and wax drippings found in the MacDonald home did not match the wax from any of the candles in the house.

Stoeckley provided a possible motive for the killings that was consistent with MacDonald's contention that the crimes were committed by members of a drug-crazed cult. Three of the members of this cult, called "The Children of Light," have now confessed. They are Helena Stoeckley, Greg Mitchell and Cathy Perry. Two of these three people, Helena Stoeckley and Greg Mitchell, were identified from artist conceptions drawn from descriptions given by MacDonald of the intruders he saw. Over thirty witnesses now corroborate the information given by the three cult members who have confessed to the crime.

During the 1979 trial, the prosecution based its case on the physical evidence found at the scene of the crime. Their strongest single piece of evidence is referred to as, "the pajama top theory," which has since been disproven, as has the prosecution's blood-typing theory, which had depended on the location of bodies and their respective blood types.

Another so-called piece of incriminating evidence against MacDonald was a bloody footprint. However, FOIA documents reveal that Hilyard O. Medlin, a lab technician had stated that there was no way to prove that the footprint in question was MacDonald's. This was because there were no lines, creases or definite positively identifying features.

Virtually all of the prosecution's physical evidence pointing to Dr. MacDonald committing the murders was purely speculative at the time of the 1979 trial and has since been disproven. The physical evidence suppressed by the government and discovered through FOIA material points to those MacDonald accuses.

A CID lab report dated April 6, 1970, reported that blood found on Colette MacDonald's hands--the hands that contained skin from her assailant--had blood type O, Greg Mitchell's blood type, not Dr. MacDonald's type B blood.

Forensic research conducted after MacDonald's 1979 trial concludes that Colette MacDonald was killed by blows consistent with a left-handed swing. Greg Mitchell was left-handed according to his wife. Dr. MacDonald is right-handed.

Other newly discovered evidence includes possession of clothing and boots by the CID which were given by Helena Stoeckley to her friend Cathy Perry so that the police would not find them in Stoeckley's possession. She eventually turned them over to Betty Garcia, a woman who had taken care of her during 1970. Mrs. Garcia turned them over to her lawyer, James R. Nance, Jr., who in turn gave the items to the CID. The CID never questioned Cathy Perry about the articles and eventually returned them to Mrs. Garcia, without ever informing MacDonald's defense team of the existence of this crucial evidence.

Additional suppressed evidence includes Army photos of the letter "G" painted on the wall of Stoeckley's apartment which matched the configuration of the letter "G" in the word "PIG" found on the headboard of the MacDonald's bed.

A bloody syringe half-filled with unknown drugs was discovered in a closet, yet never turned over to the Defense to examine for fingerprints which could well have belonged to the group MacDonald accuses.

In addition to the suppressed physical evidence and the seven key witnesses not allowed to testify at MacDonald's 1979 trial, psychiatric testimony from both a defense psychiatrist and a prosecution psychiatrist from Walter Reed Army Hospital was banned from the jury. The conclusions prosecution and defense psychiatrists reached during the Article 32 Hearings were that: "Dr. MacDonald is a sane, well-balanced adult: that he was not hiding any of the facts concerning the night of the murders and the assault on himself: that he was sane on February 17, 1970, and sane at the time of the psychiatric examinations."

In another area, it was discovered that the government was in possession of a vast amount of documentation as to the "reliability" of Helena Stoeckley as a witness, which they had argued vigorously against during the 1979 trial and subsequent appeals. These documents show that CID agents worked closely with both the Fayetteville and Nashville Police Departments with reference to Helena Stoeckley and that, for at least one year prior to, and one year after the murders, Helena Stoeckley was an outstanding, reliable informant for the police. Her information led to numerous arrests during that period of time. This means that police officers swore under oath at the time these arrests were made that their informant was reliable, and it was only on that basis that people could have been arrested on her information.

The March, 1983, issue of "The University of Pennsylvania Law Review" refers to its study of MacDonald's 1979 trial as, "How Things Should Not Work."

Since MacDonald's 1979 trial, Helena Stoeckley has confessed her involvement to three people. She confessed to Don Goldberg of the "Washington Post" and, on videotape, to Fred Bost, a North Carolina news reporter. She also confessed on videotape to Ted Gunderson, a retired special agent for the FBI, during a "60 Minutes" production. The tape has not yet aired, but is now part of the court record.

Greg Mitchell confessed to a drug rehabilitation group, and to two close friends, that he killed MacDonald's family.

Cathy Perry confessed to the FBI in the fall of 1984, that she had been present and had taken part in the MacDonald murders. According to Stoeckley, the motive for the crimes was revenge due to MacDonald's lack of cooperation in treating drug abusers with drugs. It surely has to be more than coincidence that Dr. MacDonald recalled treating a man by the name of Warmbrod shortly before the crimes were committed and that Warmbrod was, at that time, Cathy Perry's boyfriend.

An Army Major testified during the Article 32 Hearings that his first reaction when he heard about murders at the home of Jeffrey MacDonald was: "My God, the drug abusers have killed him."

Major Williams told how MacDonald, an Army doctor, counseled soldiers about drugs. And he testified that soldiers had been told at a seminar the month before the slayings, that only a chaplain had the right to keep conversations with soldiers private.

After the January, 1970, seminar, Williams testified that appointments for drug counseling dropped almost to zero and "I became very concerned not only for my health but for Dr. MacDonald's health." Both men participated in the sessions, along with lawyers and soldiers.

When MacDonald continued to talk with soldiers about sources of drugs coming into the area, Williams said, he felt the doctor, then 26, was "way over his head."

In 1970, Prince Everette Beasley was a detective with the Fayetteville, North Carolina, Police Department. He knew many in "The Children of Light" cult well. He saw two of the accused cult members shortly before the crimes were committed, and three the morning after they were committed. In a signed affidavit he states the following:

"On the night of February 16, 1970, I was on duty and parked outside the Village Shoppe Restaurant in Fayetteville. I was there in connection with my official duties, which included investigating narcotics traffic. At approximately 10:50 p.m. that night, I observed a blue Ford Mustang pull into the alley adjacent to the Village Shoppe.

Helena Stoeckley and a black male exited the car from the passenger side. Helena went into the Village Shoppe while the black male waited next to the car. Helena Stoeckley was then an informant for the Fayetteville Police Department and was providing information about narcotics traffic in Fayetteville.

"Helena was wearing a blonde wig, a floppy hat and was carrying a light colored handbag. The black male was wearing an Army jacket with E-6 insignia. I had seen the black male wearing the same jacket on numerous prior occasions. He often accompanied Helena, along with other members of the group with whom she associated.

"The following morning, February 17, 1970, I received a call from Captain J. E. Melvin regarding murders which had occurred at Fort Bragg. Captain Melvin gave a description of the suspects in the case, including a young man wearing an Army jacket with E-6 insignia and a blonde white male. Believing the persons described to be Stoeckley, Mitchell and the black male, I searched for them without success that day. Early the next morning, I set up surveillance at Helena Stoeckley's apartment.

"At approximately 2:15 a.m., on February 18, 1970, Stoeckley and two or three men pulled up in an old, faded yellow car with out of state plates. I blocked their car in the driveway with my car and called out to Helena. Before I said anything, Helena said to me that she

knew why I was there to see her and
asked: 'Mr. Beasley, do you want to see
my icepick?' I told her that I did not
think her statement was funny. I asked
her if she was involved in the Fort Bragg
murders. She said she thought she was
present when it happened, and could remember how awful it was. I radioed the
Police Department and advised them to
call the Army CID. I told them I had
found suspects in the murders. Over an
hour passed and no assistance arrived, so
I was forced to release them because they
became threatening to me.

"Two or three months after the
murders, I tried to interview Stoeckley
about the murders. She would not discuss
them with me because she was afraid of
reprisals.

"Years later, in October, 1980, after Dr. MacDonald was convicted, I began
to do investigative work on the Mac-
Donald case. In that connection, I interviewed Helena Stoeckley on several occasions concerning her knowledge of the
MacDonald murders. Those interviews occurred in South Carolina and in California.

"Helena Stoeckley stated the following: She was associated with a group
of people who were servicemen, or former
servicemen who were drug abusers, and who
dealt in drugs to support their habits.
The group was concerned about the
response of military doctors, including
Dr. MacDonald, to soldiers with drug
problems; and the group discussed re-

taliation against Dr. MacDonald because
he had refused to treat several people
for drug addiction and had threatened to
turn them in. It was decided by the group
she associated with, at some point, to
attempt to get his cooperation in helping
soldiers with drug problems, and to get
drugs from him."

"In the early hours of February 17,
1970, Helena and other members of her
group went to the MacDonald residence.
Helena named Greg Mitchell, a black male
whose nickname was Zig Zag, alias "Smitty", Bruce Fowler and Cathy Smith (now
Cathy Perry) as being present. Helena
said more than four people were there but
did not name them. She said they were all
under the influence of drugs.

"Although the group members had
mentioned killing Dr. MacDonald's family,
Helena believed that the MacDonalds' were
just going to be pushed around, but when
Dr. MacDonald put up a fight, things got
out of control, and she could do nothing
to stop it.

"She remembered standing at a couch
in the MacDonald apartment, holding a
lighted candle and remembers the hot wax
running onto her fingers. When the hot
wax burned her fingers, she extinguished
the candle and put it in her pocket.

(An Army investigator testified at
Fort Bragg that candle wax stains, found
in the apartment where MacDonald's wife
and children were slain, did not come
from candles in the apartment. Dillard
Orson Browning, a Criminal Investigation

Division chemist from Fort Gordon,
Georgia, said at a closed hearing for
MacDonald, that the stains were found on
a coffee table in the MacDonalds' living
room and on a bedspread in their daughter
Kimberly's bedroom. They did not come
from any of several candles found in the
Fort Bragg apartment by investigators.)

She saw Smitty strike Dr. MacDonald
and told him to 'hit the pig again.' She
was at that time under the influence of
drugs. She heard Colette say Dr.
MacDonald's name and ask for his help. At
some point, the telephone rang and
Stoeckley answered it. A male with a soft
voice asked if Dr. MacDonald was home.
She began to laugh, and one of the men
with her told her to 'hang up the Goddamn
phone,' which she did.

Jimmy Friar, the man at the other
end of the telephone call Helena
Stoeckley describes receiving during the
murders, was located by Washington Post
reporter Don Goldberg, who works for Jack
Anderson. In Jimmy Friar's signed affidavit, he states: "In February, 1970, I
was an in-patient at the Womack Army
Hospital in Fort Bragg, North Carolina.
Prior to February 17, 1970, I was a
patient at Walter Reed Hospital. While
there, I had gotten drunk on a couple of
occasions and needed to get help to get
back to the hospital. On those occasions,
I had called Dr. Richard McDonald (sic)
and he helped me out, either picking me
up himself or sending someone to pick me
up. At Womack Hospital, on the evening of

February 16, 1970, I persuaded an orderly
to let me out and cover for me so that I
could go to Fayetteville to drink and
shoot pool.

"When I decided to go back to Fort
Bragg, the buses had stopped running and
I had no money left to get a taxi. At
that time, I attempted to contact Dr.
Richard McDonald, who had previously
treated me, to attempt to get back to the
base. I tried to contact Dr. Richard
McDonald from the Wade Hampton Hotel. I
was disoriented at the time, and thought
I could contact Dr. McDonald by phone.
Thinking I was still in Washington D.C.,
I called the base operator and rep-
resented myself as a friend of Dr.
McDonald's.

"The operator gave me a number. I
called the number which had been given to
me and asked for Dr. McDonald. The woman
who answered was laughing, and I heard
someone in the background say, 'Hang up
the goddamn phone.' The phone was dis-
connected at that time. I made the call
sometime around 2:00 a.m. I spoke with
the FBI about this incident."

It is interesting to note that more
than several witnesses contacted the FBI
and/or the CID and either the leads were
never followed up and/or the defense was
never notified. A member of one of these
organizations, who has asked not to be
named, says it is because they are "duty
bound" to cover for their informants.

In Stoeckley's conversations with
Detective Beasley, he states that, "she

remembered seeing a rocking horse with a broken spring in the house." (The prosecution states that the picture of the rocking horse appeared in the newspaper, but what they don't tell you is that it is impossible to discern even the slightest hint of the broken spring from the newspaper picture). 'She recalled the night following the murders when I stopped her group on Clark Street. They were riding in an old cream-colored Plymouth. She said she couldn't talk to me when I stopped because she was afraid of the others. She told me that after the murders, she had given her boots and clothes to Cathy Perry to hide. Helena said she felt she had been roped into the murders and couldn't get out of it. She was still fearful for her safety and that everyone involved went into hiding after the murders."

Helena Stoeckley's husband, Ernest Davis, states in a signed affidavit that, "We were watching the news on television in August of 1979 when an announcer said something about the murder trial of Dr. Jeffrey MacDonald. Helena said to me, 'Oh, my God. The cops are looking for me now!' She told me a little about the murders and that was the first I ever heard of Dr. Jeffrey MacDonald from her.

The next afternoon the FBI came and took Helena back to Raleigh. I caught a bus down to join her. Helena had been placed in jail to keep her around to testify. I asked Dr. MacDonald's lawyer to release her and he spoke to the judge who agreed to release her providing she would promise to stay in town to testify. That night at 11:30 or 12:00, Helena sat up in bed and started scribbling on the wall and the headboard with her fingers. I asked her what she was doing and she replied, 'It's my baby!'

"After testifying, Helena told me that she acted confused at the trial in order to fool the judge. She told me that Detective Beasley had said he would try to get her immunity, but because she was not sure he could do so, she had protected herself by telling him a man named Al Mazerolle, whom she had put in jail as an informant for the CID, was involved in the murders."

Ernest Davis goes on to state that, "She said she went into Dunkin' Donuts the night of the murders with blood on her hands and she washed them there. She would come up with things that would make you believe she was there, because they were things that no one else would know.

"We were walking in Greenville one day when we passed a rocking horse on the side of the road. Helena started crying. She pointed out that the spring was broken just like the one in the MacDonald house.

"Helena told me that she remembered driving to Dr. MacDonald's with other people and parking. She told me she remembered going into a bedroom to keep the kids quiet. When she came out, she said MacDonald was already stabbed and Colette MacDonald was screaming. The next thing she remembered was standing in the living room, holding a candle. Blood was dripping off of her hand.

"Helena also told me that somebody went into the jewelry box in the MacDonald house and took some things out. Helena told me that everybody was scared and wanted to get out of there, and they all left in a hurry, leaving all the weapons behind, except for a pair of scissors. They went to the donut shop and cleaned up. When Helena got home, her roommate asked her why she did it. Helena replied, 'They deserved to die.'"

Edith Boushey, an English teacher who taught at the North Carolina State University Extension program at Fort Bragg, North Carolina, recalls seeing members of the group MacDonald accuses on the first floor near the front of the entrance of the building where she taught. She says: "I particularly recall three of the women in the group because of their manner of dress. One woman wore an off-white floppy-brim hat, a three-quarter length vinyl coat and clean white boots. A second woman was dark-haired, and a third woman wore a beret and a white vinyl coat. I have viewed a sketch of a blonde woman wearing a floppy hat (an artist's rendering from the description given by MacDonald), and I can identify this woman as one of the women present at the school on February 16, 1970.

"I also observed a woman and a young man standing apart from the group. I did not recognize the woman at the time. However, I recognized that woman as Colette MacDonald in photographs printed in the newspaper later during the week of February 16, 1970. Colette MacDonald was wearing a camel-colored coat. She appeared troubled and worried. The man who was speaking with Colette MacDonald was white and was wearing a clean, well-kept Eisenhower field jacket, khaki pants and Army boots. He was approximately 5'9", tall and slender. He had a fair complexion, reddish brown hair, small, striking blue eyes and fairly chiseled features. I have also looked at photographs and sketches in order to identify the man who was speaking to Colette MacDonald. I selected a sketch which resembles the man I saw that evening."

The sketch Edith Boushey selected was an artist rendering of Greg Mitchell, from a description given by MacDonald. Edith Boushey says she reported her observations to two Army investigators within the first week after the murders. And although they came to her office at the school, they never asked her any questions regarding the murders or the suspects. She also furnished what she had witnessed to an FBI agent in the Spring of 1970.

Another witness, Frank Boushey, confirms seeing the group MacDonald accuses at Dunkin' Donuts the evening of February 16th at the same time Helena Stoeckley told her husband they were there.

Two additional witnesses, Marion Campbell and her husband, also identified the group as being there that evening.

John Humphries, a former Military Policeman and a member of the Police Reserves, saw a group on February 16, 1970, in a rock shop he owned. In Humphries' signed affidavit, he states: "The next morning I read about the MacDonald killings in the paper. On the way to work, I stopped to get gas and told the attendant that I wouldn't be surprised if these people were the ones who did it because they were hippies and all doped up."

He remembered them because they had come into the filling station in a van, at about midnight to get gas. He said he was quite scared of them and had reported them to the police. "When I got to my shop, I called the FBI and told them what I had seen. I never got a response from them. I also called the CID at Fort Bragg but received no response from them either. The filling station attendant received no response to his call either."

Richard Comisky states that he personally knew Helena Stoeckley and ran into her in a Fayetteville Park between August and October of 1970. In his signed affidavit he states, "We began speaking about insignificant things when Helena Stoeckley said, 'We did the MacDonald thing.' I asked her what she meant and she said, 'We did the killings.' The man with her told her to be quiet but she reassured him that she had known me for a long time and it was okay to speak in front of me. The man told her to 'be cool and not put their business on the streets.' During the course of the conversaion, Helena asked me whether I knew if fingerprints could be obtained from wax. I told her I did not know whether they could or not."

Debra Lee Harmon states that a week after the MacDonald murders, she was sitting in Rowan Park waiting for a drug dealer when Helena Stoeckley and her group sat down near her. When the drug dealer came, she said he warned her to stay away from that group because, "They were the individuals responsible for murdering the MacDonald family."

At the end of August, 1979, after MacDonald's conviction, Lynn Markstein was involved in a traffic accident in Raleigh, North Carolina. As a result of the accident, she went to Wake Memorial Hospital. Helena Stoeckley was there for treatment of injuries received as a threat to testifying in the MacDonald case. Lynn Markstein states that, "Helena Stoeckley introduced herself to me and told me she was in Raleigh to testify at the MacDonald murder trial. Helena Stoeckley told me that she was at the MacDonald house at the time the murders occurred. She said she remembered standing over a child in a bed. The child was uncovered. Stoeckley said that blood was all over the child. I remember Stoeckley making the statement, 'Can you imagine someone like me doing that to those babies?'"

Helena Stoeckley stated that Greg Mitchell was the one who murdered Colette MacDonald. Ann Cannady is one of several witnesses who corroborates Stoeckley's statement that Greg Mitchell was involved in the murders. She says, "During March of 1971, a thin young blond man came to The Manor looking for a place to stay. On the Saturday after he arrived, he came to the regular Saturday night session attended by those staying at The Manor. He said that he was part of a cult that worked together and confessed that he had been a drug user and that he had murdered people. On the following Sunday morning, he was gone from The Manor. Late on Sunday, I went with Reverend Phillips to the farmhouse The Manor operated in the country. As we pulled up the road to the farmhouse, we saw the young man who had made the confession on Saturday night run out the back door. We called the Sheriff's Department. When the Sheriff's Deputy arrived, we went through the house with him. We walked into the bedroom which adjoined the living room and saw written in bright red paint on the wall, "I killed MacDonald's wife and children."

Mr. and Mrs. Bryant Lane also signed affidavits stating that they clearly heard Greg Mitchell directly admit his involvement in the murders.

Other new witnesses heard implicit admissions from Harris and Smitty. They overheard the group planning the murders at a local restaurant and were able to recall the movements of the Stoeckley group on February 17 and in the following months.

Additionally, an ex-MP saw three of the men, one identified by a photo, running through the bushes near the Mac-Donald home, minutes after the murders.

In summary, there is now concrete physical evidence which supports MacDonald's recollection of the crime scene. There are three confessions from people who knew each other and were involved in the same drug cult. Two of these three people were identified from artist conceptions drawn from descriptions given by Dr. MacDonald of the intruders he saw. In addition, there are over 30 witnesses who now corroborate the information given by the three people who have confessed to the crimes.

The mentality of those responsible for sending MacDonald to prison and keeping him there is similar to that of those who sent and kept Dreyfus imprisoned on Devil's Island. This mentality is quite well expressed in a letter sent to Dreyfus after he was freed by one of his "before and after" comrades at the General Staff Offices in France. The letter states:

"When the Deputy Chief of the General Staff gathered us in 1894 to tell us that you were guilty and that they had undisputable proof, we accepted that certainty without discussion since it came

to us from a superior. In that context,
we immediately forgot all your qualities, the friendly relations we had with
you, in order to search in our memory
only for what might corroborate the certitude that had just been inculcated in
us."

ALFRED G. KASSAB
AMERICA'S MOST COSTLY
IMMIGRANT

5

Alfred Kassab, responsible in large part for MacDonald's imprisonment, is known to his friends and enemies alike as Fred or Freddie. Born in Montreal of wealthy parents, he was sent to school in both France and the Mid-east.

When the war started in 1939, Kassab joined the Canadian Army and states that he was assigned to its field security force. Kassab left the Army in 1944 and immigrated to the United States in 1946. Kassab met Colette MacDonald's mother, Mildred, in 1956. It was not long until they married and went on a honeymoon cruise to Europe.

Both Mildred and Fred Kassab approved of Jeff MacDonald from the very beginning, and were delighted when Colette and Jeff were married in a small Greenwich Village Church on September 14, 1963.

The Kassabs' feelings about Jeff and Colette's life together are best stated in Fred Kassab's testimony at the Army Article 32 Hearing, which took place shortly after the murders. The questions Kassab was asked and his answers are as follows:

Q. Would you state your full name and address for the record?

A: Alfred Kassab, 22 Bonnie Lane, Stoney Brook, New York.

Q: Would you spell your last name please?

A: K-A-S-S-A-B

Q: Would you state what relationship, if any, you are to Captain Jeffrey R. MacDonald.

A. I am his father-in-law.

Q: And were you the father of his wife, Colette MacDonald?

A: Yes, sir.

Q. Were you her natural father?

A: No, her stepfather.

Q: May I ask when you and Mrs. Kassab were married?

A: Fourteen years ago.

Q: And how old was Colette MacDonald at that time?

A: Twelve.

Q: And how long did Colette MacDonald live in the Kassab family home with you and your wife?

A: As long as we were married, fourteen years.

Q: When did you first come in contact with Jeffrey MacDonald?

A: About twelve, eleven, twelve.

Q: How did you meet Captain MacDonald?

A: I met him in--now, my wife--she wasn't my wife--I met him at her home as he was visiting my daughter.

Q: And over the next few years, did you have occasion to see him again?

A: Oh, quite often.

Q: What high school did your daughter attend?

A: Patchogue High School.

Q: Patchogue, Long Island, New York?

A: Right.

Q: And do you know what high school Captain MacDonald attended?

A: He also attended Patchogue High School.

Q: During the years that your daughter was in high school, did you ever have occasion to see Jeffrey MacDonald?

A: Yes, quite often.

Q: Would you describe to the investigating officer the circumstances and how you came to see Captain MacDonald during that period of time?

A: Well, Captain MacDonald used to come and see my daughter and there was a period in there where they were on the outs, and Captain MacDonald still used to come to our house, and he used to mow the lawn in the summertime and shovel the driveway in the wintertime, regardless of the fact that they weren't going together and he'd stop by every once in a while and leave a gift on the back steps and leave.

Q: How often would you say you saw Jeff

MacDonald during high school years?

A: About once a week, at least.

Q: Was your daughter actually in a boy-friend girlfriend relationship with him part of that high school period or all of that high school period?

A: Most of it, yes.

Q: Now you indicated that Colette and Jeff were on the outs at some time. Are you indicating that there were some arguments or strong disagreements between them?

A: No, I think it's probably one of those teenage things that happens to most young people in their 15 to 16 year age group, right in there somewhere.

Q: Were there any violent arguments that were between them at that time?

A: Never to my knowledge.

Q: Did you ever hear Jeff MacDonald raise his voice to your daughter in anger during that period of time?

A: Never at any time.

Q: Never at any time? Are you referring to the entire period...

A: From that day to this day.

Q: How well did you come to know your step-daughter?

A: Well, I would say that Colette and I were as close as anyone could possibly be with his own natural daughter.

Q: What was--did your relationship with Colette include her discussing things that troubled her or problems that were on her mind?

A: At times, yes.

Q: Was she a child who shared her concerns or anxieties with you and her mother?

A: Well, not completely, I would say. No, she didn't. She--if she had any problems that we didn't know--well, I will say that if ever she had a problem and she didn't tell you about it, you could see it on her face. It would be apparent in her voice immediately.

Q: Was she the kind of person who could hide from you?

A: Absolutely not.

Q: I'm referring to her real emotions or--

A: She wasn't capable of it.

Q: Did she tend to try and suppress her real feelings about situations from you?

A: No, I don't think so. I don't think it was a matter of suppression. I think it was that--I had never known her to have any problems particularly, but I would just venture to say that had she had a problem, that, as I said a few minutes ago, I would have known it immediately. But with her, it would have been a matter of, if she had a problem, she would have related it. She didn't like to--if she had a problem, say in school with her studies, of that type, she wouldn't come out and say it, but you could tell that there was something wrong.

Q: Now were your step-daughter, Colette, and Jeff MacDonald of the same age?

A: Yes, sir, within a month, I think.

Q: What year was Colette born in?

A: I--I don't have it off the back of my head.

Q: That's all right. Now when your daughter graduated from high school, what did she then do with herself?

A: She attended Skidmore College, Skidmore University in Saratoga Springs.

Q: New York State?

A: Yes.

Q: And do you know what school Captain MacDonald went to?

A: Yes, he went to Princeton University.

Q: Did Colette and Jeff continue to have any contact during the period of time that she was at Skidmore and he was at Princeton?

A: Well, I know from Colette that she had spoken to Jeff and corresponded with him the first year. And the second year they were going together.

Q: And when you say in the second year that they were going together, what do you mean by that?

A: They were boyfriend and girlfriend relationship.

Q: Did Colette have occasions to come home to Long Island during vacations or weekends at all?

A: Yes, she'd always come home weekends, most weekends that she had--when she felt she could come down and she could afford it.

Q: And did Captain MacDonald ever visit

your home during his early college
years?

A: Yes, sir.

Q: And what was the nature of the relationship between Jeff and Colette
at that time?

A: Boyfriend and girlfriend.

Q: Now when did they marry? In what
year of their college education?

A: The second year after. At the end of
the second year, if I am not mistaken. I may be wrong there. It
could have been at the beginning of
the third year. It was right in
there.

Q: And when they married, where did
Colette MacDonald then go to reside?

A: In Princeton.

Q: Did you have occasion to visit your
step-daughter and son-in-law while
they were married and together at
Princeton?

A: Yes, sir, I did.

Q: On more than one occasion?

A: On two occasions.

Q: Did they have occasion to visit with
you?

A: Yes, they came to visit with us. I
couldn't say how many times, but I
know I went to Princeton with my wife
twice.

Q: What did you observe about the
relationship between Colette and Jeff
when they were first married and
living together at Princeton, New
Jersey?

A: Well, they were like a couple of pigs

on ice. I'll put it that way as an expression. They had a home. It was a very large home. Ah... since they were--Jeff was struggling through college, they rented this very large house and had maybe seven or eight bedrooms and they acted as chaperones weekends for girls coming to visit boys at the University, and readied up beds, and this helped to pay for their rent.

Q: From what you are saying, could you give us some indication of what their financial status was during that period of life?

A: Well, it was very close for, you know, Jeff was getting loans from the bank to pay for his college education, and it is pretty hard for a man working his way through college all on his own.

Q: In addition to the money they earned from renting out the beds in their house, was there any other way that either Colette or Jeff was earning money during that period of time?

A: Well, Colette babysat for one, and Colette also typed papers for other students, and they earned money that way.

Q: Now how long was Captain MacDonald at Princeton University after they were married?

A: Three years.

Q: No, after they were married?

A: No, it was over two years, and not three years.

Q: Then Captain MacDonald left Princeton after three years there?

A: Yes, sir.

Q: And where did he go then?

A: He went to Northwestern University in Chicago.

Q: Did he go there as an undergraduate?

A: Yes, sir.

Q: Undergraduate school or medical school?

A: Medical school.

Q: And did Colette MacDonald go with him and set up housekeeping there?

A: Yes, sir.

Q: Where did they live when they were at Northwestern?

A: They took an apartment, the address I don't know.

Q: They had an apartment in the Evanston area?

A: I don't know this.

Q: Did you have occasion to visit with Colette and Jeff while he was in medical school?

A: Yes, sir.

Q: Did the MacDonalds come to visit you in Long Island on any occasions?

A: Yes, sir.

Q: What did you observe about the nature of their relationship at that time while they were in medical school?

A: It was no different at that time than it was at any other time. They were happy.

Q: Had the MacDonald's children been born at the time they were in medical school?

A: One was born, yes.

Q: Which one was that?

A: Kimmie, Kimberly.

Q: And was the second child born while they were in medical school?

A: Yes, sir.

Q: Now did the addition of the first child appear to add any stress or cause an emotional strain to show on Colette or Jeff?

A: No, sir. Colette wanted five.

Q: Wanted five children?

A: That was always her statement.

Q: What was her attitude toward her first child in terms of her feelings?

A: For actually being a mother for the first time, I don't think anybody could be happier. Let's put it that way.

Q: Was the second child a child that was wanted at the time it was had?

A: Absolutely.

Q: Did you observe Jeff relating to his children while he was in medical school?

A: Yes, sir.

Q: Can you describe his attitude and conduct toward his children?

A: Well, to the best of my knowledge, let's put it this way--to my knowledge, whenever I was present there, he would actually spend more time with the children than he did with either myself or my wife because of the fact that his time was completely taken up with studies, and any time he was in the the living room, he would be playing with the children, and at the same time was talking to us.

Q: Now after Jeff graduated from North-western Medical School, where did he go?

A: He went to Columbia University to serve in--Columbia Presbyterian Hos-pital to serve his internship.

Q: And did they live in the New York area?

A: In New Jersey, local Jersey, right a-cross the bridge from New York.

Q: Did you and your wife have occasion to see Colette and Jeff during that period of time of the internship?

A: Yes, and my wife more frequently than I. My wife would go over at a min-imum of two or three times a week.

Q: Did the MacDonalds have occasion to visit you at Patchogue on Long Is-land?

A: Yes, sir.

Q: What did you observe about their re-lationship during that period of time while he was interning at Columbia Presbyterian?

A: It was, as I said before, their relationship never changed at any time that I ever noticed.

Q: When you say it never changed, what was that relationship? How would you describe it?

A: To the point where they were really an exceedingly happily married couple, and the second child seemed however, they seemed to be happier yet.

Q: Now when Jeff finished his internship at Columbia Presbyterian, where did he go?

A: The day he finished his internship, he reported to the Army in Texas.

Q: And do you know approximately how long he was in Texas?

A: It seems to me it was four weeks, but--

Q: Thereafter, where was he assigned?

A: In Georgia, I think, at the jump school.

Q: Fort Benning?

A: That could be it. I'm not sure.

Q: And following jump school where was he?

A: He came here.

Q: Fort Bragg?

A: That's right.

Q: Now when did Mrs. MacDonald join him, join her husband in the military service?

A: I drove her down here myself. If I'm not mistaken, it was in October of last year. The exact date --

Q: October 1969?

A: Yes, sir.

Q: Did you maintain contact with Jeff and Colette when they were both together here at Fort Bragg?

A: Yes, sir. I called on a minimum of once a week.

Q: Did you speak with your stepdaughter during that period of time?

A: Yes, sir.

Q: Did you have occasion to visit them

here?

A: Yes, sir. Well, aside from the first time when I brought her down here with the children, my wife and I were both down here last Christmas, for Christmas.

Q: December 1969?

A: Yes, sir.

Q: Did either Jeff or Colette have a chance to visit you on Long Island during the period they were home from Fort Bragg?

A: Captain MacDonald did, yes, sir.

Q: When was that?

A: He came back for a weekend on business, personal business of some kind, and he stopped in to say hello to us. But his wife wasn't with him.

Q: How long were you here at Fort Bragg in December of 1969 with Colette and Jeff?

A: It was either three or four days.

Q: And would you describe for the investigating officer how your daughter seemed to be in terms of her married life, married relationship?

A: Well, I would say that even though I've used ecstatic expressions to prior times, I think they were considerably happier here than they had ever been.

Q: And why was that?

A: Well, I would think that it would be the less financial problems from the point of view that they had a home. They—Jeff came home most nights, which he'd never been able to do be-

fore. He had more time to be with
the children, more time to devote to
Colette, and they seemed to--of
course you can imagine a wife with a
husband in internship and medical
school gets to see not too much of
her husband. Here she saw him almost
every night and she was ecstatic
about it.

Q: Did anything of an unusual nature
happen during your Christmas visit
here at Fort Bragg?

A: Yeah, this was well, not unusual.
Christmas morning, at about six
o'clock--I'm an early riser--I was up
walking around and Jeff said to me,
'I've got a surprise,' he said, 'for
the kids for Christmas, and I want
you to come down and take a look.' So
he and I got dressed and left the
house before my wife and daughter and
grandchildren got up, and we drove
down the road three or four miles
here, and he showed me a pony that he
had bought for the children.

Q: Did anyone know about that?

A: No one but me.

Q: No one in the house?

A: Not in the household. I think if I
remember correctly, a fellow officer
on the base helped them to build the
lean-to that they had built for the
pony.

Q: And what happened when you went down
to visit the horse?

A: Well, we went to where the horse was
being kept and when I saw the horse,

I thought it was terrific for the children--pony, I should say--and then we went back to the house, and Jeff proceeded to tell Colette that he had ordered a gift for the children for Christmas and that Sears-Roebuck fouled it up--but there was one in the window and if we'd all get in the car, we'd go down to see this thing so at least they could see what they were getting for Christmas. And we drove down the road and then we turned off and Colette didn't understand why we were turning off the road and not going straight down to Sears-Roebuck, and he said, 'Well, I gotta stop here and pick something up.' And we drove down to the corral and we all got out of the car, and he said, 'I want you to see something over here,' and we took them over there and showed them the pony.

Q: What was Colette's view of the gift for the children?

A: To the best of my recollection, she cried for half an hour.

Q: Now when did you leave your step-daughter and son-in-law in December?

A: It was the day after Christmas.

Q: Did you--what was her attitude as far as family relationship at the time you left her?

A: They were very, as I say, they were the happiest I've ever seen them.

Q: When you indicated that Colette cried on seeing the horse, was that--as far as you could tell--was that because she was sad or disappointed?

A: No, Colette being, always was a very sensitive child, and anything that made her very happy, she cried.

Q: Did you then have contacts with your stepdaughter and son-in-law between December and February 17, 1970?

A: Yes, sir, I called, as I said before, a minimum of once a week, sometimes twice, and as a matter of fact, I spoke to her the Friday prior to February 17th, and on February the 15th, although I didn't actually talk to her, I was on the other phone while my wife was talking to her.

Q: So you overheard the conversation?

A: Yes, sir.

Q: How did your daughter seem to you when you spoke to her on the very last date, that February 15th--Sunday evening?

A: During the day sometime, yes. She sounded no different than she had ever sounded.

Q: Did you--did she give any indicatiion that there was any marital problems between herself and Captain MacDonald?

A: None whatsoever.

Q: Did she give any indication that she was having any difficulty with the children?

A: No sir.

Q: Did she give any indication that she was suffering from a depression from her pregnancy?

CPT. SOMMERS: I object to this. He has--he is leading much too much. I object to that question.

MR. SEGAL: It relates to a specific characteristic. I think we can understand what we are dealing with here.

CAPT. BEALE: The objection is overruled.

A: No. Let me back up on that question and answer you from this point of view--that I have stated previously that my daughter had expressed her wish for five children, and that this one was her third and she was ecstatic about the idea, even though she knew and I knew that her having children was a very dangerous thing.

Q: Why was that?

A: Because she'd had two prior Cesareans, and the last one, in Chicago, if it hadn't been for Captain MacDonald she would have died in the recovery room.

Q: Would you describe the incident to the investigating officer?

A: Well, that incident was related to me by both my daughter and Captain MacDonald. I wasn't there, but she had been--the Cesarean had been performed and that she was in the recovery room, and since Captain MacDonald had access to the hospital as a medical student, he went in to visit her in the recovery room, and upon entry he found that she had hardly any pulse and no blood

pressure whatsoever, and he went
quick and got the surgeon and they
operated immediately again and saved
her life. There had been--something
happened to one of the blood ves-
sels--I'm not really being technical. I really don't know what happened, something along this line had
happened.

Q: Did Captain MacDonald ever have occasion to express to you his feelings about the marital relationship
at the time you saw them in December,
or in any way show you his feeling?

A: Well, the man spent most of his time
playing with his children all the
time that he was home. Every time
you turned around, he had one of the
girls playing with him. At
least--let's put it this way--more so
than most people I know of. He spent
more time with them than most people
I know.

Q: Did it in any way appear to you that
he was neglectful and not attentive
to his wife, your stepdaughter
Colette?

A: No, sir, he spent--well, he was the
type of man that, who had come home
at least once a week with a gift of
some kind.

Q: For whom?

A: For my daughter, and I would say that
he bought, personally all by himself,
approximately 80 percent of her
clothes as surprises for her.

Q: What was Captain MacDonald's attitude

towards the Army and his service in
the Army?

A: Well, Captain MacDonald, to the best
of my knowledge, from talking to him
and seeing his deportment, he was exceedingly proud of belonging to the
Green Berets.

Q: By the way, have you ever served in
the Army, sir?

A: Yes, sir.

Q: What was your--

A: I was in the Canadian Army in World
War II.

Q: How long were you in the Army, sir?

A: I was with the Canadian Intelligence,
Military Intelligence.

Q: Were you an American citizen or a
Canadian citizen?

A: I was a Canadian citizen.

Q: And are you a Canadian citizen now?

A: I am an American citizen.

Q: When did you become an American
citizen?

A: I moved to the United States in 1946
and became a citizen in 1948.

Q: If Captain MacDonald was free to
leave Fort Bragg today, would you accept him into your home, sir?

A: Yes, sir.

MR. SEGAL: Cross examine?
WITNESS: May I add one thing to
that?
MR SEGAL: Yes, you may.
WITNESS: If I had another
daughter, I'd still want the same
son-in-law.

COL. ROCK: Let's recess for five minutes.

The murders were understandably difficult for both families to accept and hardest of all for MacDonald, who had lost the family that was everything to him.

At the Army base in Fort Bragg, North Carolina, where the funeral took place, Mildred Kassab, MacDonald's mother-in-law, quite understandably spent most of the time secluded in her room. The Army bent over backward to please her, even to the point that, when Mildred claimed the Army's dishes were not fit for her to eat from, she and her husband, Fred Kassab, were finally offered the General's china!

With the exception of MacDonald, all the Kassabs' hopes and dreams had literally turned to ashes. This was clearly communicated to their mutual friends in a discussion about Colette's brother Bob, when Mildred said, "If only it had been Bobby's family."

Kassab, like everyone on MacDonald's defense team, was very upset about the Army's handling of the investigation of the murders, and wrote a letter to the Army with the following complaints:

"The Military Police officer in charge the morning of the murders, refused a request by one of his sergeants to seal off the base and question everyone leaving. I had been told by Colonel Kriwaneck that this had been done immediately.

"One hour after the murders, at approximately 5:00 a.m., CID agents admitted that there was a civilian in the house wandering around. He had long hair and was wearing dungarees. They swore that no one thought to ask him who he was or what he was doing there. Furthermore, they did not know when he arrived nor when he left.

"Captain MacDonald's wallet, which appears in an Army photo taken at approximately 5:00 a.m., had disappeared by 6:00 a.m.

"A CID agent, Robert Shaw, when questioned as to what was done with the many sets of fingerprints that could not be identified with any person ever known to have been in the house, and were they sent ot the FBI lab in Washington, D.C., for comparison with their files, replied, 'I didn't know the FBI performed that service.'

"It was apparent from footprints found in the master bedroom that Kimberly, my eldest granddaughter was there when her mother was being attacked, yet she was found in her own bedroom. In regard to this, the following fantastic statement was made by a CID agent, 'When hippies kill someone they let the body stay where it falls. They don't move it.'

"After much prodding by the defense, the Army admitted that my daughter's jewelry box had blood on it and unidentified fingerprints. It also came out that they didn't think to ascertain whether any jewelry was missing. Two rings my wife had given Colette, which were family heirlooms, were missing. It was established at the hearing that no one had thought to take an inventory of the contents of the house, and as of the end of the hearings, it still had not been done.

"Two women neighbors of my daughter testified that they had heard voices of at least two men and a girl, going in the direction of my daughter's backyard immediately prior to the murders. They also stated that they had given this information to the CID, but that they did not seem interested. At this juncture, I should point out that many persons called the defense lawyers with information on possible leads to the murderers. They stated that they all had called the CID offering to give them the information, but no one had ever come to question them or asked them to come into the CID office (this information is all documented).

"The defense brought in a civilian witness who identified a composite drawing of the girl Captain MacDonald had described. She lived next door to him. He stated that during a conversation with her one day after the murders, he asked her if she and her boyfriend were going to be married. Her answer was, 'We have to prove ourselves first and kill a lot more people.' This witness told the court that the girl had a large floppy hat, a blonde wig and high boots such as Captain MacDonald had described and that she had disposed of these items on the day of the murders. A reporter for the "Fayetteville Observer" tracked the girl down and she admitted to him about disposing of these garments. When he asked her where she was on the night of the murders between midnight and 4:00 a.m., she said that she was so high on drugs that night that she does not remember anything.

I was at Fort Bragg when this testimony was given. I first went to the Army Provost Marshall's Office and demanded protection for the witness, who was in fear for his and his wife's lives, also that they pick the girl up for questioning. They refused on the grounds that these people were civilians and did not come under their jurisdiction. I then went to the FBI where I got the same answer, 'lack of jurisdiction.' When I asked, "Who should I go to?" I was told the Army, since the local police don't have jurisdiction either.

"The girl Captain MacDonald described was carrying a lit candle during the murders. Only after insistence by the defense did the CID admit that candle drippings had been found in various rooms. Further arguments ensued before the prosecution would produce lab reports on the drippings. It turned out that the chemical analysis showed that the drippings did not come from any candle in the MacDonald house.

"The most shameful thing of all was the presentation by the Army of the autopsy reports. Normally, these would be given verbally by the doctor who performed them. Not in this case! They brought in a projector and a large screen and over defense objections, they forced Captain MacDonald to sit through autopsy pictures of his family.

"In the middle of the hearings the defense took the Army to Federal Court and asked for a sworn statement that the Army was not wiretapping phone conversations between Captain MacDonald and his lawyers. This the Army refused to do.

"Now to the hair sample episode. A strand of hair was found in my daughter's hand. The Army insisted in the middle of the hearings that it was imperative to their case that they have samples of Captain MacDonald's hair, due to the fact that the samples they had, which had been labeled, 'Known Samples of Captain MacDonald,' turned out to be horse hairs. He told them that if they got his commanding officer to give him a direct order, he would obey it, but no, they would not do that.

"One day, between the courtroom and the cafeteria on the base, seven jeeps and two civilian cars full of MP's and CID men ran his car off the road and, without provocation, beat up one of his lawyers and slammed the other against the car. This shameful episode was witnessed and photographed by newsmen on the scene. Later, this was called a cheap publicity stunt by the U.S. Attorney in Fayetteville who, by the way, happens also to be the legal advisor to the Army on Civilian matters.

"They took Captain MacDonald and got hair from various parts of his body, this was on July 20th. Then, silence. Every day the hearing officer, Colonel Warren Rock, would ask in court, 'Do you have the results of the hair tests?' The answer was always 'No.' Finally, his patience ran out, and early in September, he demanded that the report be produced in court the next day. It turned out that the hair did not match. The head of the CID, Franz Joseph Grebner, finally admitted that they had received the report from the lab on approximately August 5th, but somehow it got into his safe, and he forgot about it due to other pressing matters.

"The Army's basic case was as follows: They didn't believe Captain MacDonald because the coffee table was lying on its side and that this was an impossibility.

"They claimed that they had experimented over a hundred times, but that no matter with what force the table was hit or pushed, it always fell on its top, because they said it was top heavy. Also, that with only the kitchen light on, the Captain could not have seen the faces of the murderers as he had claimed. Colonel Rock, the presiding officer decided to see for himself, so one night after dark, he went to the house accompanied by his legal officer and the head of the CID. The first time he kicked the coffee table, it landed on its side. He then lay on the sofa, with the two men at the foot and only the kitchen light on. Colonel Rock stated that he could clearly see the faces of both men."

Kassab now says that when he lay on the same couch in the same postion and under the same lighting conditions as MacDonald had, he could scarcely make out figures standing in the same place as those MacDonald accuses, conveniently overlooking the findings of Colonel Rock, who states the following: "I simulated the lighting conditions as per the accused's testimony. From a prone position on the couch, the length of which I noted, I was able to discern the facial features of Captain Beale at the end of the couch."

MacDonald states that Colette cried out to him for help. Kassab questions how Colette could have called out for help when her trachea had been cut. MacDonald's testimony states that he was awakened by Colette's screams for help. This statement indicates that the screams must have occurred early on in the attack, making it likely that Colette's cries for help came before her trachea had been cut.

In other testimony, MacDonald states that he regained consciousness on the hall floor after being attacked while attempting to save his family. Kassab now asks why there was no blood found on the hall floor--this question, despite the fact that he states he read and re-read the Article 32 Hearing transcript in which an MP testified that there was blood on the hall floor.

In another instance, MacDonald testified that he was at the kitchen sink either before or after he used the kitchen phone. If it was before, Kassab now asks, why was no blood found at the sink? If it was after, Kassab asks why there was no blood on the phone? Here again, he ignores the Article 32 Hearing transcript in which an MP testified that MP's thoroughly cleaned the sink in order to make coffee and that an MP wiped the phone clean before using it to call headquarters.

Kassab claims he withdrew his support of MacDonald because evidence he discovered in the Article 32 Hearing transcript caused him to suspect MacDonald's guilt. However, since the massive Article 32 Hearing document served as the basis for the Army's exoneration of MacDonald as the perpetrator of the crimes, this then leaves a large question as to the real motive behind Kassab's crusade to have MacDonald convicted for the murders of his wife and two children. A crusade which has ruined the life of a doctor whose biggest ambition is to save lives. A crusade which has taken more American tax dollars than any other legal case in our country's history, making Alfred G. Kassab indeed, America's most costly immigrant.

124

After reviewing the evidence shortly after the murders occurred, Kassab stated to the press: "We know full well that Jeffrey MacDonald is innocent beyond any shadow of a doubt, as does everyone who ever knew him."

Some say that though the Kassabs had been good to Colette, MacDonald, and the children, they had strong feelings of guilt and remorse over not having given as much of themselves as they could have throughout the years when Colette and MacDonald were building their family. Just days before the murders occurred, Colette had asked her mother whether she and the children could come for a visit, and had been refused because of other activities that were keeping Mildred and Fred Kassab busy.

There was also an on-going disagreement between the families due to the importance Mildred Kassab placed on material possessions.

Jeff and Colette's will reads that, "Upon death of both in a common catastrophe, we nominate, constitute and appoint Dorothy MacDonald to be the guardian of our children." This statement must have been a bitter pill for the Kassabs to swallow.

In addition to the contradictions previously stated, Kassab says in a letter to the Congress that the CID admitted there was blood on Colette's jewelry box and that there was foreign candle wax in the house. Kassab now denies these and numerous other documented facts in statements he has made to the press.

In fact, he has even gone so far as to state that Jimmy Proctor was not Judge Dupree's son-in-law, despite the fact that even Judge Dupree admits this. Upon being asked if he received money for his involvement in "Fatal Vision," Kassab states that he did not receive anything...despite the fact that his agent says that he received $25,000.

No doubt, just as some of the officers who became relentless in their hostility to Dreyfus turned into fanatics--Kassab in turn has grown fanatical in his belief of MacDonald's guilt--and now seems unable to distinguish between truth and lies, fact and fiction. Perhaps the murders have grown to become too much for him to endure.

THE PLIGHT OF A COUNTERFEIT JOURNALIST'S DESTINY

6

If Jeffrey MacDonald had read Joe McGinniss' book, "Heroes," there never would have been a book entitled "Fatal Vision."

In "Heroes," McGinniss tries to sell his readers a bill of goods which says there are no heroes in the world. In fact, as you study the history of McGinniss' career, you will find that it has thrived on his evil protrayal of our country and its heroes.

Barres, a French author who fought for Dreyfus' innocence, states that, "this kind of demi-culture attitude destroys instinct without replacing it with conscience."

In a chapter of "Heroes," in which he tells of his childhood and parents, McGinniss describes himself as his mother's "treasure, her angel, her pride and joy." Yet in the more than five thousand words he takes to describe his parents, he cannot seem to find one kind word to say about them. This attitude, I believe, provides a strong insight into the serious flaws lurking in McGinniss' character...or rather the lack of it.

One of the "heroes" McGinniss befriended was George McGovern, who enjoys the reputation of a bright, honest, hard-working statesman. In regard to an article McGinniss wrote about McGovern, McGovern says, "The article is full of inaccurate and fabricated quotations. In my twenty years of public service, I have seldom encountered a more disreputable and shoddy piece of journalism."

Kathleen Hall Jamieson's book, "Packaging the Presidency," adds fuel to McGinnniss' reputation as a counterfeit journalist. In one particular instance, Nixon campaign strategists Shakespeare, Price and Garment reviewed approximately seven hours of Nixon on film and concluded that he came off best when he was spontaneous. The "Man in the Arena" concept derived from this conclusion was created to bring out Nixon's spontaneity. However, in McGinniss' book "Selling of the President" the incident was designed to show that Nixon's advisors first decided what image would sell, and then contrived to create and sell that image...the exact opposite of what, in fact, took place.

"Fatal Vision" reeks of situations in which McGinniss reports the exact opposite of what actually happened, despite the fact that he was in possession

of complete documentation on the Mac-
Donald case.

Like Kassab, McGinniss is confident
the public will believe whatever he says,
and repeats Kassab's erroneous statements
that (1) there was no blood found on the
floor of the hallway where MacDonald had
been found lying facedown and unconscious
after having been stabbed in the chest,
despite Military Police testifying at the
Article 32 Hearing that there was blood
found in the area where MacDonald had
lain unconscious just before awakening to
search the house for his family. (2) no
fingerprints were found on the telephones
MacDonald used to call for help, despite
an MP testifying that before using the
phone to notify headquarters that they
had arrived, he wiped the phone clean.

In still another example of McGinniss
writing the exact opposite of what actually took place, he states in "Fatal
Vision" that MacDonald refused a sodium
amytal interview. The Grand Jury record
confirms, however, that MacDonald agreed
to the interview. It states on Pages 77
and 78, "this is to acknowledge your
telegram dated January 23, 1975 received
by me on behalf of the Grand Jury today."
The telegram reads:

From: Bernard L.Segal 1/23/75.
To: Mr. Epperson, Foreman of Grand
Jury, Raleigh, N.C.
cc. Victor Worheide

We urgently request that Dr. Sadoff
be allowed to testify in person con-

cerning the psychiatric examination he made of Dr. MacDonald within a few weeks after the death of his family. Dr. Sadoff advises me that he will be available to testify before you between February 3 and February 21, with reasonable notice of the date he is wanted. If it is appropriate for the work of the Grand Jury to be held up for four weeks while a government attorney goes on vacation to Europe, then the Grand Jury has a right not to be stampeded in proceeding without Dr. Sadoff's personal testimony.

The testimony of Dr. Sadoff will also be important because he has advised me that Dr. MacDonald is able to undergo a sodium amytol interview. This interview will be completed by February 3 and Dr. Sadoff will be in a position to report personally to the Grand Jury on the results of that interview. It would be unforgivable of the government's attorneys to block this direct and personal testimony on a subject which the members of the Grand Jury have stated firmly they want to hear about. There is no legitimate reason for the Grand Jury not to hear Dr. Sadoff's testimony in person concerning his psychiatric examination of Dr. MacDonald and the results of the sodium amytol interview which will take place shortly.

(We agreed to the sodium amytol interview at the urgings of the Grand Jury and now only ask that the Grand Jury hear in person the results of that interview.)

Despite McGinniss' statement to the contrary, it is clear MacDonald agreed to the sodium amytol interview. This kind of vicious deceit continues to flourish throughout "Fatal Vision." For instance, McGinniss says that MacDonald's residency at Yale was withdrawn, yet I received a copy of a letter dated July 7, 1970, from Wayne O. Southwick, Chairman of Orthopedic Surgery at Yale, which states the opposite. The letter reads as follows:

"Dear Jeff:
I am sorry that I have not written to you sooner regarding your decision to withdraw from the residency program. I am deeply sorry that you do not feel able to go ahead at this time, but I certainly do understand. The world has, indeed, dealt you a difficult blow and I only wish that I could do something more to help you counter your life and your career. Jeff, I have no regrets or no apologies to make to anyone about our relationship and I take considerable pride in the fact that you were planning to come here to train with me. I only hope that you will be able to reconstruct your life so that you can achieve what you truly deserve."

The letter is signed, "Most sincerely, Wayne O. Southwick, M.D."

In another instance, McGinniss goes on to spend a great deal of time giving credence to the government's hypothetical "pajama top" theory. However, in McGin-

niss' letter of December 18, 1979 to Mac-
Donald he states the opposite. Here, Mc-
Ginniss agrees with his friend Boyd Norton, a former nuclear physicist, who says
he is astonished that such "hocus pocus"
could be admitted as evidence in court.

Boyd Norton, McGinniss related, was
"amazed and appalled at the way much of
the 'scientific' evidence was assembled,
verified and presented in court. He suggested that the defense should have a major league scientist "to review the physical evidence and come up with so many
flaws in methodology and deduction as to
invalidate any conviction based upon such
material."

In editing McGinniss' manuscript,
Phyllis Grann, publisher and editor-
in-chief of G P Putnam's Sons, states in
a letter dated November 4, 1982, to
McGinniss that, in regard to the pajama
top: "The reader should believe that this
evidence proves Jeff's guilt." Whereas
McGinniss' book contract states that he
is obligated to maintain the essential
integrity of MacDonald's life story, it
is clear neither he nor Grann had any
intention of doing so, and depended upon
MacDonald's guilty verdict to support
McGinniss' lies.

In Grann's letter of November 4,
1982, to McGinniss, she goes on to state
that the "reader is certainly left with
the impression that Mildred (Kassab) will
lie to get Jeff convicted. Wouldn't it
be better to close this chapter with some
comment of your own?" When it comes to

"hocus pocus" McGinniss has indeed proven himself a pro.

In "Packaging the Presidency's" account of McGinniss' interpretation of Nixon in "The Selling of the Presidency" it is clearly obvious that McGinniss ignores indisputable evidence that runs counter to his case. Jamieson states that "some evidence of selective reading can be gleaned from McGinniss' treatment of the questions and answers between Nixon and local radio commentator, Jack McKinney, on a Philadelphia panel show. It is McGinniss' belief that Nixon ducked the tough questions of the national press by instead holding highly orchestrated panel shows using citizen interviewers. 'He would not allow himself to be questioned by professional questioners, only under circumstances where his own people would pay for an hour.'"

McGinniss told David Frost. "They would pick the panel themselves, and then they would put him up live and say, 'Here's Nixon answering Americans' questions'." That is the charge McKinney makes. To McKinney's question, McGinniss reports this response from Nixon:

"'I've done those quiz shows, Mr. McKinney. I've done them until they were running out of my ears.'" There was no question on one point: Richard Nixon was upset. Staring hard at McKinney, Nixon grumbled something about why there should be more fuss about Hubert Humphrey not having press conferences and less about him and "Meet the Press." In the control room, Frank Shakespeare punched the palm of one hand with the fist of the other and said, "That socks it to him, Dickie baby!" The audience cheered.

What McGinniss neglects to report is the substance of Nixon's answer. The "Washington Post's" account of the exchange reads: "McKinney noted that Humphrey had questioned why Nixon had not appeared on "Meet the Press", "Face the Nation" or "Issues and Answers" for almost two years. Nixon replied that he had been on those 'quiz shows until they were coming out my ears.'" He said he was doing something that was much more difficult in holding formal press conferences for the reporters accompanying him on his campaign. Nixon had held three formal press conferences that month.

He asked why Humphrey had held no such press conferences on his campaign, except for an informal session during a beach walk in New Jersey last week. So McGinniss is guilty of dropping from his report Nixon's answer, information that would rebut one of McGinniss' central claims. Newspaper accounts confirm that Nixon was indeed holding press conferences. Additionally, Don Irwin, the "Los Angeles Times" reporter assigned to Nixon's campaign, confirms that Nixon did have press conferences at the stops! McGinniss plays this same game in excerpts entitled, "The voice of Jeffrey MacDonald."

Nixon advisers prove time and time again that McGinniss selected judiciously from their conversations and in his subject matter magnifies the manipulation he sees and manipulates the magnification.

"Broad inferential leaps from evidence that when taken in context more readily bears an alternative reading" runs rampant in "Fatal Vision." In one instance, McGinniss states that fibers from MacDonald's pajama top were found under Colette MacDonald's body. What he doesn't state is that both a photographer and a doctor testified that they had, in separate instances, moved Colette's body.

In another instance, McGinniss' description of Kristen MacDonald's wounds does not match up with the autopsy report. The autopsy report states that ten of the wounds in Kristen's chest formed an elongated "S" pattern. McGinniss' translation of the autopsy report neglects to mention this point, which is key because Helena Stoeckley, who had admitted to being present at the scene of the murders, had stated to a number of witnesses that the "S" stood for Satan, a fact McGinniss also left out.

In yet another obvious attempt to destroy MacDonald's character, McGinniss describes a trip MacDonald took from the East coast to California. McGinniss says MacDonald travelled with a 16 year old girl and that they had sexual relations throughout the trip. It turns out though, that the 16 year old girl was accompanied by her mother, her brother and the family dog and all deny any sexual relations took place.

To augment McGinniss' character assassination of MacDonald, he creates an amateurish theory which concludes that an overdose of dextro-amphetamine (a diet pill) drove Dr. MacDonald to the murders. What McGinniss doesn't tell his readers is that the Army considered amphetamines dangerous drugs in 1970 and tested for them in Army hospitals routinely as a part of their anti-drug campaign. MacDonald's medical records state that he was tested for all drugs and that not so much as a trace was found in either blood or urine tests. Had McGinniss told the whole story he would have clearly disproved his own theory. *See page 285.*

The same holds true with much of the physical evidence--evidence which, had McGinniss been motivated to do his homework, would have proved MacDonald could not have committed the murders.

Had McGinniss looked, he would have found at least 45 pieces of evidence indicating intruders were in MacDonald's home the night of the murders. Through CID reports he would have discovered evidence of a struggle everywhere. Had he talked to Major James Williams at Ft. Bragg, he would likely have learned that the Army had a motive for covering up the crimes of the confessors to the murders of MacDonald's family. And he would likely have discovered that the confessors were government informants involved in illegal LSD experiments at Ft. Bragg.

Instead, perhaps McGinniss was too

involved in his own motive: that of creating a best seller in order to bail himself out of bankruptcy. He sensationalized and fictionalized incidents to fascinate the reader. He created a non-existent motive, and fraudulent prose to make his story believable.

In a letter dated April 14, 1982, McGinniss writes, "I still plan to finish the whole book by Spring--remember Spring lasts until June 21--and as soon as I've finished--even while I'm going through as many hoops with publishing lawyers as you are with Spritzer and the Segal family. Sterling can start to negotiate first serial and foreign rights, as well as overseeing the movie situation.

"It better happen that way, and fast, because I'm at rock bottom, financially, and don't even have a condo at Mammoth I can unload."

McGinniss' letter of May 16, 1983, to MacDonald states:

"In addition, knowing that I have no money now, knowing that, in fact, I owe the Bank of New York $20,000 and Nancy's father $15,000 and my mother $5,000 (I'm not shitting you--times are tough); and having himself (Sterling Lord, McGinniss' literary agent) loaned me $9,000 over the past several weeks, Sterling agreed to refund half of his original commission from the Dell deal. No one to whom I have spoken as this was going on has ever before heard of an agent doing such a thing."

McGinniss stated to MacDonald in his

letter of September 11, 1979: "It's a
hell of a thing--spending the summer
making a new friend and then the bastards
come along and lock him up. But not for
long, Jeffrey, not for long."

And on September 28, 1979, he wrote:
"...It seems to me that one very
important benefit of the book is that it
gives you something constructive to do
day by day. Something real: something
valuable: something essential. A way to
channel your anger and reflections. A
book about the case: no convict should be
without one. Even in jest, it doesn't
feel right to type the word 'convict' in
reference to you and I am hoping like
hell this phrase will come to as quick
and merciful a halt as possible next week
in Richmond with the granting of bail.

"Jeff, it is still very hard to accept all this. To have you writing about
prison...

Goddamn, Jeff, one of the worst
things about all this is how suddenly and
totally all of your friends--self in-
cluded--have been deprived of the pleasure of your company.

"So, even as imperfectly as I have
expressed it, what I mean is I am still
sorry as hell this whole thing ever
happened, and I am impatient to see you
again and to plunge into the book, and,
hopefully, once again to share with you
many laughs and good stories and new experiences as well as re-living, in sor-
row, some of the bad ones from the past."

On November 2, 1979, McGinniss wro-

te: "Jesus, you have a lot of decisions
to make. I sure hope you get to make them
from the comfort and privacy of your
home."

All the while McGinniss was writing
letters to MacDonald, he professed loyalty and close friendship to him. McGinniss now states, in a brief defending
himself against the fraudulent activities MacDonald accuses him of, that
he agonized over the tragedy with which
he was presented. McGinniss states of
MacDonald: "He was a human being crying
out in anguish. I cared for him, the way
I care for a lot of my friends..."

MacDonald obviously believed McGinniss cared for him. In his letter of
April 27, 1982, to McGinniss, MacDonald
states: "I'm sane, angry, scared. They'll
throw away the key unless I win soon." In
MacDonald's letter to McGinniss of August
22, 1982, he says: "I hope you understand the depth of my despair and anguish..."

Clearly, however, McGinniss was not
the friend he pretended to be. Instead,
the following letter from McGinniss to
his first editor, Morgan Entrekin, dated
November 3, 1981, portrays McGinniss as a
Judas. Here McGinniss states: "I spoke to
him (MacDonald) last night and he kept
referring to 'our book' and was astounded
that Taylor-Wigutow could have given a
story to the "Hollywood Reporter" to the
effect that they were planning a film on
Dr. Jeffrey MacDonald 'convicted of having murdered his wife and children,' when

the whole point of film and book, obviously was that he was falsely convicted, as he had been falsely suspected for ten years, etc. etc. He's letting this one pass: writing it off to the sloppiness of a trade paper, but the ice is getting thinner and I'm still a long way from shore."

In McGinniss' quest for further character assassination and sensationalism, he develops a theory that MacDonald is the victim of "pathological narcissism". McGinniss quotes from a 1975 book written by Otto Kernberg, a psychoanalyst who discusses the narcissistic personality. Kernberg says, according to McGinness, that the main characteristics of narcissistic personalities are "grandiosity, extreme self-centeredness and a remarkable absence of interest and empathy for others in spite of the fact that they are so very eager to obtain admiration and approval..."

An innocent reader, having no first-hand knowledge about MacDonald would assume, through McGinniss' calculating cleverness with words, that MacDonald possesses these traits. Those who know him are adamant that the opposite is true. They all concur that self-centeredness and an absence of interest and empathy for others are clearly foreign to his mental makeup. The lifelong friends he grew up with say, "He was always so popular because you knew he cared about you--there was no question, and that if you had a problem and he could help, he would."

Anthony Abbate, Vice President of the Los Angeles Hospital Council, says he has not come in contact with a more competent, empathetic and trustworthy doctor in his entire career.

Police Officer Jim Fortier says, "If you need someone to run through crossfire to save an injured man, you call Dr. MacDonald. He has a respect for life and the preservation of it like no one else I know. That's why we appointed him the first honorary lifetime member of the Long Beach Police Officer's Association."

John Rambo, an ex-professional basketball player, who organizes sports for underprivileged children in Long Beach, California, says: "Dr. MacDonald was always there when you needed him. The kids trusted him because he was gentle, intuitive and just plain fun. He knew how to motivate them to take good care of themselves, he taught them how. Dr. MacDonald hasn't been with us for awhile now. You can tell the difference, but what you really can't know is how much we need him back."

Dr. Seymour Halleck, a Duke University Psychiatrist who examined MacDonald stated on William Buckley's, "Firing Line," that the author's "pathological narcissism" theory was "amateurish." He goes on to say that according to the official nomenclature of the American Psychiatric Association, there is no such mental malady as pathological narcissism. Dr. Halleck concludes that the theory is a concoction fueled by the author's imagination and that McGinniss has no background competent to create a motive for the kind of person MacDonald is.

In a "Philadelphia Inquirer" interview dated November 18, 1984, McGinniss stated to reporter David Bianculli, "Never have I told anybody anything untrue in order to get information." Here again, he leaves himself wide open.

According to Kathleen Jamieson's "Packaging the Presidency," Nixon aide, Len Garment, approved McGinniss' proposal for a post-graduate thesis, but not for a book entitled, "The Selling of the President." McGinniss lies when he says, "Never have I told anybody anything untrue in order to get information."

In another instance in which he wrote a letter to MacDonald, dated May 30, 1980, he says, "Don't be bashful. I am the only one who hears these tapes and beneath this cynical exterior beats a sentimental, gullible, Irish heart." After receiving confidential tapes from MacDonald, which speak of private, intimate encounters between him and his girlfriends, the man with the "sentimental, Irish heart" transcribed the tapes word for word for all interested parties in America and the world to read. After meeting several of the girlfriends McGinniss described, I was frankly astounded to discover that they were bright, sensitive, wholesome and well

educated. McGinniss' talent for "creating images that do not comport with reality" makes them appear as brainless,
clinging "off-the-street" mistresses,
further degrading their true character,
as well as MacDonald's.

With no evidence to support the
accusation, McGinniss calls MacDonald a
pathological liar; yet you begin to wonder whether McGinniss isn't a pathological liar when you read McGinniss'
letter of September 20, 1979, to Mac-
Donald. In this letter he sets out to
persuade MacDonald to discourage any writer other than himself from writing a
book or articles on MacDonald. He says
of his rival, Bob Keeler, "Keeler's story
is going to have a hero, and guess what,
it isn't going to be you." According to
McGinniss' statement that he made up his
mind when the jury made up theirs that
MacDonald was guilty, it was actually in
his own book that MacDonald would not be
the hero, and he knew it. On the other
hand, there is no evidence to this day
which indicates Keeler had decided upon
MacDonald's guilt or innocence.

"Philadelphia Inquirer" reporter
David Bianculli also states that McGinniss' later statements often conflict
with earlier ones. McGinniss states on
more than one occasion that he made up
his mind about MacDonald's guilt the day
the jury made up their minds. However, in
a letter to MacDonald dated September 11,
1979, he states: "Total strangers can
recognize within five minutes that you

did not receive a fair trial. My lawyer
from Princeton, who knew only what he
read in the N.Y. papers, commented that
it sounded to him as if you'd drawn a
real bad hard-line southern judge and
when that combines with a southern jury,
however well educated, anything can
happen. Even if you are not black. (You
are, of course, from California, which
apparently is almost as bad)."

He also stated that he made up his
mind when Helena Stoeckley testified.

Yet in a letter to MacDonald dated
December 18, 1979, he says: "One certainly gets the impression that Colonel
Rock was a more impartial and intelli-
gent hearing officer than Judge Dupree."

To Bianculli he states that he made
up his mind "by Spring or early summer of
1980." McGinniss goes on to state that
his friendship with MacDonald disappeared
rather promptly after his decision about
MacDonald's guilt, yet there are numerous
friendly letters from McGinniss to Mac-
Donald, some dated as late as May 3,
1983, and May 16, 1983.

It is highly suspicious that Mc-
Ginniss knew from the very beginning that
he was going to write a "bad" book about
Jeffrey MacDonald, no matter what the
verdict. Why else would he have insisted
MacDonald insert a clause in the contract
which states, "I will not make or assert
upon you any claim or demand based on
the grounds that anything contained in
the book defames me."

In a letter to MacDonald, McGinniss

writes: "I'm glad in the midst of all the
turmoil, you haven't forgotten those releases re: Ma, Jay Judy. There are so
many insane lawsuits flying around in all
phases of publishing and movies these
days that you literally have to submit
copies of the necessary signed releases
along with the manuscript to all mag-
azines, movie studios and foreign pub-
lishers. (Sterling, incidentally, thinks
the foreign market for this book will be
very big)."

Following is a copy of the Consent
and Release between MacDonald and Mc-
Ginniss:

CONSENT AND RELEASE

For and in consideration of the sum
of One Dollar ($1.00) and other valuable
consideration paid to me, receipt whereof
is hereby acknowledged, I hereby irre-
vocably grant to Joe McGinniss ("you")
and to any party authorized by you
(whether or not you receive consideration for such authorization) and to
any party succeeding to you, interest in
these presents:

1. My consent and the right forever
throughout the world to use, publish,
exhibit and exploit all interviews with
me, in whole or in part, in books or
other publications, in motion picture and
television productions, (including, without limitation, by so called "pay",
"free", "free home", "closed circuit",
"theatre", "tool", "CATV" or "subscrip-

tion television" and by the use of cart-
ridges, cassettes, discs and other de-
vices similar or dissimilar and by any
other process of transmission now known
or hereafter to be devised and in any and
all other similar and dissimilar media of
any nature whatsoever and in the production, promotion, distribution, sale,
rental, advertising and publication
thereof, which may be based in whole or
in part on my life (with the unlimited
right as you may in your sole discretion
deem proper, to quote directly, to para-
phrase, to edit, to rewrite, to add material to and/or delete material from and
otherwise to make use of such recording
and other reproductions and interviews);
to describe, impersonate, simulate,
depict, and portray me under my own or
any fictitious name, and use my name and
to make such use of any episodes of my
life, factually or fictionally; in any
and/or all of the aforesaid media as you
may in your sole discretion deem proper; and to combine such description, im-
personation, simulation, depiction, por-
trayal and episodes and uses with
descriptions, impersonations, simu-
lations, depictions and portrayals of,
and episodes from the lives of, other
persons factual or fictional; to do any
or all of the foregoing in exercising and
exploiting any and all further rights in
any and/or all of the aforesaid media.
    2. My consent and the right to
copyright (in the United States and anywhere else) for initial and any renewed

or extended period of copyright in any name or names whatsoever, all such interviews, and any and all such books and other publications and any and all productions in any and all of the aforesaid media.

3. I hereby agree that you and any party authorized by you or succeeding to your interest in these presents may exercise all or any of the rights herein granted by me without claims, demands or causes of action, whether for libel, defamation, violation of right or privacy, or infringement of any literary or other property right or otherwise, insofar as I am concerned.

4. Without limiting the foregoing, I agree that all of the consents and rights herein granted to you shall be exclusive and perpetual throughout the world."

Fortunately for MacDonald, Bernard Segal, his lawyer at the time, inserted a clause which said: "Provided that the essential integrity of my life story is maintained."

This clause was ignored by McGinniss, and Susan Baerwold, NBC Vice President of Docudramas, who states in regard to "Fatal Vision": "We made a deal with a reputable writer. I knew that anything that would be published in the book would have to be substantiated." She made a very serious error in judgment.

MacDonald's fraud suit against McGinniss, is best detailed by MacDonald's civil attorney, Gary L. Bostwick, in the "MacDonald Newsletter," Vol. 2, May, 1985. In it, Bostwick writes:

"Dr.Jeffrey MacDonald has filed suit against Joe McGinniss, the author of "Fatal Vision," in the United States District Court in Los Angeles, California, for damages totaling 15 million dollars. Dr. MacDonald has also asked the Court to order McGinniss and his agents to account for all monies received by McGinniss from "Fatal Vision" and all of its by-products. Over the course of the next two years, the scenario of the litigation will be played out in California, Texas and New York to determine whether McGinniss defrauded Dr. MacDonald during the four long years of investigation and research on the book.

When the allegations of the complaint are boiled down to their essence, what remains is a simple claim. Dr. MacDonald is suing McGinniss for leading him to believe that he was conducting research and investigation for the original book with an open mind and an objective passion, when in fact he had already made up his mind that the conclusion of the book would point toward guilt. The suit alleges that Dr. MacDonald entered into a written agreement with McGinniss in July, 1979, shortly before Dr. MacDonald's trial in North Carolina. Dr. MacDonald was induced to enter into the contract because of his urgent need to defray the costs of defense. He also had a burning desire to have the full and true story of his family's tragedy told in an effective manner. The allegations of the suit set forth the following contentions:

> Dr. MacDonald allowed McGinniss entry into his most intimate confidences and provided McGinniss with information and access to personal files, family, and friends. McGinniss was even allowed to move into the living quarters where Dr. MacDonald, his lawyer and family lived and worked during the trial. McGinniss' expenses during that period were covered by Dr. MacDonald.

McGinniss has stated publicly that he became convinced that Dr. MacDonald was guilty of the charges against him during the trial. However, McGinniss kept his conclusion to himself at all times and did not communicate this to Dr. MacDonald or any of his attorneys or friends. For four long years, Dr. MacDonald continued to believe that McGinniss was convinced of Dr. MacDonald's innocence and the certainty of his ultimate exoneration of the crimes of which he was charged.

However, during the four years that followed the trial, McGinniss continued to deceive Dr. MacDonald in order to obtain free access to personal books and papers, intimate tape-recorded reflections and recollections, and papers and materials stored in Dr. MacDonald's home.

The complaint also alleges that much of "Fatal Vision" is false and McGinniss knew that he was fabricating certain portions of the book when he wrote it. The fictional falsities have been repeated in numerous interviews with newspapers and on television. (Attorneys for Dr. MacDonald complained to NBC before airing of the mini-series based on "Fatal Vision" that the screenplay preserved great numbers of McGinniss' inaccuracies.)

Dr. MacDonald has also alleged in his complaint that he has not received a correct and prompt accounting for all of the monies that have been paid to McGinniss or his agents for the book and its film successor. One allegation is that McGinniss:

> "entered into unusual agreements with NBC that arranged for him to be largely paid under a special consulting contract rather than under a royalty contract, thereby avoiding the need to account for his earnings and to share them with Dr. MacDonald."

McGinniss has mistakenly stated that Jeff complains that McGinniss promised to write a book proclaiming his innocence. It does not allege that. What it does claim is that McGinniss coldly misled Dr. MacDonald by failing to tell him that he had already made up his mind that he was guilty before even beginning the bulk of

his investigation. Dr. MacDonald coop-
erated in every way with McGinniss only
because he believed that McGinniss had an
open mind. Dr. MacDonald also refrained
in large part from granting interviews to
other authors who may have wanted to
write the true story of the events. He
did so because he believed that Joe
McGinniss was writing just that: an unbiased story.

Attached to the complaint are
several letters from McGinniss to Dr.
MacDonald laced with McGinniss's sometimes profanely uttered protestations
against the unjust system that could
result in a conviction, sometimes pro-
fessing the great pain McGinniss felt at
being deprived of Dr. MacDonald's company, frequently offering advice (regarding even attorneys, appeals and bail)
urgently asking Dr. MacDonald's help in
collecting information for the book and
aid in preventing others from writing
competing books and articles.

The letters themselves, contrasted
with the statement publicly made by Mc-
Ginniss that he had made up his mind in
July, 1979 as to Dr. MacDonald's guilt,
provide the most accurate picture for any
reader or jury seeking to determine how
the fraud was perpetrated.

All of the above matters will
obviously require presentation of hard
evidence at trial. The case is in its
early stages, on the eve of further production of documents as well as depos-
itions of key witnesses, including Dr.

MacDonald and Joe McGinniss themselves.
Joe McGinniss has stated to "TV Guide"
that his publisher is paying for his
defense fees in this case. Dr. MacDonald
has no publisher to rely upon. In one of
the letters attached to the complaint,
McGinniss told Dr. MacDonald:

> "The fact is you lost the
> case, you are now in prison, you
> may be out on bail within days,
> you may be freed on appeal within
> months, you may be tried again,
> or, though it scares me to even
> type it on paper, the thought has
> surely crossed your mind--none of
> the above may come to pass and you
> would have to serve your sentence
> until paroled. In all honesty,
> Jeff, this last seems to me by far
> the least likely of possibilities.
> Conviction in this trial, however,
> seemed by far the least likely
> possibility, too. What I'm get-
> ting at, I guess, is that you
> ought not to make life any more
> difficult for yourself than it al-
> ready is by re-hashing trial tac-
> tics over and over again, fruit-
> lessly. It is bail, about which,
> essentially, you can do nothing,
> and the appeal process, about
> which you could do a great deal,
> which should receive the bulk of
> your energy and attention. And,
> of course, the book, toward which
> we will have months and months to

work together."

McGinniss worked those months and months without ever telling MacDonald that he had become convinced of his guilt long before writing the words set forth above.

Dr. MacDonald's position throughout the litigation has been and will continue to be that it was unfair and unjust for McGinniss to hide his conviction while leading him through four years of co-operation on a book that ultimately would trumpet that conviction in a best seller and movie made for television."

Not only did McGinniss perpetrate a fraud, he has violated the very principles of a newsman's responsibilities. As stated in "Playing it Straight, a Practical Discussion of Ethical Principles of the American Society of Newspaper Editors," Hulteng (The Globe Pequot Press, 1981), at 5:)

> "The primary purpose of gathering and distributing news and opinions is to serve the general welfare by informing the people and enabling them to make judgments on the issues of the time. Newspapermen and women who abuse the power of their professional role for selfish motives are faithless to that public trust.

> "It is difficult to imagine a more egregious violation of that trust

than that committed by Joe Mc-
Ginniss in investigating and writing "Fatal Vision."

Fraud in fact (criminal fraud) is
defined as deceit, i.e. concealing something or making a false representation
with an evil intent when it causes injury
to another. McGinniss' fraudulent acts
also include taking money which lawfully
belongs to MacDonald. To date, MacDonald
is missing his share of payments from
disbursements of the proceeds of "Fatal
Vision" for $50,000, $6,000, $3,257,
$4,000, $130,000 and a portion of a
$248,836 disbursement, plus all dis-
bursements made after MacDonald filed
suit against McGinniss.

McGinniss attempts to shift the
blame for monies MacDonald is missing to
the man who helped to bail McGinniss out
of bankruptcy--his agent, Sterling Lord.
Yet Sterling Lord was able to produce a
letter dated October 31, 1984, from
McGinniss which states: "The business
part of this letter is to formally in-
struct you, as my agent, to cease immediately, and until further notice from
me, the remission of any further "Fatal
Vision" payments to Jeffrey MacDonald."

McGinniss' motive becomes fairly obvious when you read his comment to
Bianculli regarding McGinniss' counter-
suit for "Not less than $100,000" claim-
ing MacDonald can't sue him (despite the
fact he did). Here McGinniss says, 'What
he's done himself is the one thing I

could never do; he cut off his money.'
Money, in McGinniss' own words, is the
name of the game he played.

Perhaps there's another underlying
reason McGinniss committed these dis-
graceful acts. The clue is in his book,
"Heroes". In describing his childhood,
McGinniss implies that he has a desperate fear of being a "loser." Can it
be that only by destroying someone else
he can feel like a hero?

McGinniss certainly has a history of
attempting to destroy every hero he
writes about. So far, all of McGinniss'
heroes have survived, though MacDonald's
future is in question. As for McGinniss'
destiny, it may simply be that of a loser, or at best, a counterfeit journalist.

WAR AMONG THE PATRIOTS

7

CHAPTER VII
WAR AMONG THE PATRIOTS

Dreyfus' patriots were quite different from MacDonald's patriots. Whereas MacDonald's patriots are primarily comprised of family, friends and support ers from all walks of life, Dreyfus' patriots, referred to as "Dreyfusards," were primarily comprised of teachers, lawyers, journalists and parliamentarians, professionals who fought for Dreyfus in terms of a political cause for the good of France. The advantage to Dreyfus was that this group was savvy to the workings of France's political system. Their education and experience allowed them to unite in order to create a viable campaign to free Dreyfus and restore him to his rightful place in life.

The key to their campaign was to present all of the evidence supporting Dreyfus to the public at one time, rather than in bits and pieces. The result was a tremendous impact, which rendered the French government almost helpless. The government simply could not effectively

fight the overpowering rage of the public
over the injustices dealt Dreyfus and,
after a brief time, had no choice but to
free him.

Unlike Dreyfus' patriots, MacDonald's patriots are at a disadvantage in
that, as a group, they are not atuned to
the inner workings of our country's political system. Rather than uniting in a
campaign to free MacDonald, many, for
lack of direction, spend valuable time
and energy fighting with each other over
unimportant shortterm goals, not the
least of which is, how to attract Mac-
Donald's attention to themselves. To be
fair, some of this infighting is caused
by MacDonald's competitive spirit and his
unique charm and charisma--all of which
was clearly lacking in Dreyfus, who had
an introverted "lack-luster" personality,
making his patriots almost purely
interested in his cause for justice, rather than in him as an individual.

Jeffrey MacDonald is known to his
patriots as "The Rock," because he never
seems to lose his composure and can be
counted upon to come to the rescue in
times of crisis, despite the terrible
tragedies he continues to experience.
All of the patriots want a piece of "The
Rock," and some of those who have a piece
of the rock, spend endless time jockeying
for position to get a bigger piece. Those
who have no piece often attempt to knock
others out of position in order to claim
the territory.

Although MacDonald does not believe

this to be true, I find that his Army of old friends (those who knew him before his 1979 trial), often band together to try to keep his new friends from trespassing into their territory. This promises to be an endless battle, because MacDonald is out-going. He is genuinely interested in people, and has a unique way of making those he meets feel good about themselves. This, in turn, makes for very good feelings toward him. Unlike the majority of us, he puts up no front, exuding an open charm that draws people to him, bringing an endless parade of new patriots into his life. Hence, the old patriots are constantly at war with the new patriots to protect their piece of "The Rock". Sometimes the old patriots tend to forget that MacDonald has a lifelong history of being loyal to his friends and would never forget them, intentionally ignore them or desert them in their time of need.

It is generally agreed that with Colette, Kimberly and Kristen gone, MacDonald's mother, Dorothy MacDonald, (called Perry by her friends), holds claim to the biggest piece of "The Rock".

As MacDonald is often described as the All-American boy, his mother can best be described as the All-American mother. Since her children's teenage years, she has experienced one tragedy after another, beginning with the death of her husband from lung disease at a very early age. Shortly thereafter, came the the death of her son Jeff's family: then the

CID named him the chief suspect in the murders.

During this time period, her older son Jay's sometimes unstable mental condition worsened. Rapidly following these events was the slow deterioration of her own health--which has accelerated much more quickly since the guilty verdict was reached at MacDonald's 1979 trial. Through it all, Perry MacDonald has remained dedicated to her family. She makes every effort to help meet the needs of Jeff, his brother Jay, and sister Judy. Perry MacDonald is a very strong person mentally, and though she cannot understand why the tragedies and injustices have not ended after all these years, she remains determined that one day her family will have a happy life together again.

Jeff's brother Jay has shown great promise in diverse areas of the business world. Though a big success in his earlier years, particularly at school, he does not seem to have the mental strength to cope with some of the more stressful aspects of his life. This situation likely stems from his extremely idealistic attitude about how the world around him should function.

Jay's first mental breakdown occurred when Jeff and his family were at the height of their happiness. His troubles have since been compounded as a result of MacDonald's tragedies. MacDonald has made all possible efforts to help Jay make a life for himself. He has obtained the best medical and mental professional help for Jay. He has also made an effort to find jobs for Jay that suit his capabilites; not an easy proposition, because although Jay is smart, he does not always stand up to the stresses inherent in most of the positions that would fully utilize his superior intelligence. Jay is exceptionally kind, thoughtful and giving to his family and friends in circumstances that do not put him under pressure. He is an excellent cook and a warm attentive host. To the joy of his many less talented friends, he is a whiz at home repairs, remodeling and other areas of the construction field.

No doubt Jay is not alone in having a difficult time coping with the world as it is today. Jay states simply that he should have lived in a different time and place...a place that functions by utilizing its natural wonders.

MacDonald's sister, Judy, is described best by those who know her as a vivacious person--one who is very bright, quick-witted, and vocal in her opinions. She is attractive in the "All-American" sense, and popular with her family and friends. The injustices dealt her brother have put a damper on her life and on the lives of her two children. But like MacDonald and their mother, she is a survivor. Judy keeps in close touch with MacDonald, but tries not to get overly involved in his case because it is too painful an experience to cope with on an every-hour basis.

Judy was very close to Colette, and often reminisces about the good times they had together. High on the priority list of MacDonald's pet peeves is smoking. Colette and Judy used to delight in seeing how many cigarettes they could smoke without MacDonald catching them in the act. When Judy visited them, she and Colette would smoke in the bathroom and other out-of-the-way places. Between the two of them being very clever, and MacDonald being very trusting, I don't believe they ever got caught. Judy marveled at what a great mother Colette was and laughs about her lack of housekeeping talents. After all, she says, "No one is perfect."

Several years ago, one of the largest chunks of "The Rock" was taken by MacDonald's ex-fiancee, Randi Dee Markwith. When I first heard about Randi, I assumed she had taken MacDonald for better and left him for worse, shortly after his bail was revoked and he had returned to prison.

In organizing MacDonald's memorabilia, however, I came upon a mountain of correspondence from Randi to MacDonald. I had promised him that I would not read any of his personal letters, and have kept that promise. However, it was necessary to read return addresses and bits and pieces of postcards to see who wrote what, when, so that some semblance of order could be created.

In addition to the return addresses

on envelopes from Randi were the most wonderful messages to MacDonald. They were full of love and wit, sparkling with such enthusiasm, I will never believe that she didn't mean every word of every message--all of which communicated very clearly to me, that despite her break-up, she was head-over-heels, madly in love with MacDonald.

I have a feeling that MacDonald was as crazy about Randi as she was about him. Randi, by all accounts, is sensationally attractive, and though MacDonald states that they didn't have many of the same interests, they were the same, in ways unique unto themselves. Their energy and enthusiasm levels would be hard for anyone to surpass, and they had the kind of carefree fun together that is usually a once-in-a-lifetime experience.

MacDonald married Colette at an early age, and though by all accounts he was happy, it is clear that he missed out on the happy-go-lucky years most of us have before we marry. While others were playing, MacDonald was working. While many of us were still receiving allowances from our parents, MacDonald was supporting a family while attending first, Princeton, then medical school at Northwestern, and finally Columbia Presbyterian, where he completed his internship.

MacDonald had several serious girlfriends before Randi came along, but none of them had Randi's ability to make him abandon some of his cares and woes and enjoy the fun he had missed out on for so many years. It is apparent that Randi kept MacDonald on a high that will be a real challenge for anyone else to match. She, and only she, broke down the wall he had built around his feelings. Sadly, it has been built up again, stronger than before.

MacDonald claims that his relationship with Randi went from "incredibly good" to "nothing, zero" when he was locked in solitary confinement at Lompoc for 55 days, during his seemingly endless journey to Bastrop, Texas. What happened to them? It's possible that even he and Randi don't know. I feel, however, that there was trouble brewing from the start of their relationship, because Randi took a large piece of "The Rock."

The impression I have is that most of MacDonald's friends and family highly resented Randi, and though MacDonald heatedly denies that this is the case, intuition tells me that they were suspicious of her motives and jealous of her charm. They felt inadequate, left out, and in some cases, downright abandoned. The old friends, I surmise, banded together in a campaign against Randi, claiming: Randi was too young. MacDonald was robbing the cradle. Randi didn't have his best interests in mind. She manipulated him. And though MacDonald states that he and Randi used to joke about the way she manipulated him, he seems to resent attempts to be manipulated more than almost anything else. Hence, "manipulation" was likely a cleverly calculated criticism, particularly when connected to the accusation that Randi talked MacDonald into buying a condominium in Mammoth and, in fact, kept him all to herself up there. From the way MacDonald talks about the wonderful (though short-lived) times they had together in Mammoth, it seems to me as if their time there was just what the doctor ordered.

Manipulation is a natural talent inherent in successful people. The art of manipulating often brings about positive results and is usually present in close relationships. Perhaps the reason MacDonald is put off by manipulation, is because he has had a definite overdose of manipulation from both his friends and his enemies. Interestingly, he is a prime target for manipulation because he is so incredibly naive about some aspects of life.

It has been stated that Randi left MacDonald, but in reality, it may be more likely that she was very cleverly manipulated out of his life at a time when she and MacDonald were both at their most vulnerable. MacDonald had recently been thrown back into prison--a particularly horrifying event for an innocent man who thought he was free.

It was up to Randi to support MacDonald during this crisis, which she did, until the break-up. But who was there to support her? MacDonald's friends made a grudging attempt for his sake. In all probability though, she knew how they really felt about her and so, in reality, she had no one to lean on. She needed someone, and she found someone. It isn't likely she planned that it would turn into a romance, but it did, and MacDonald found out about it, I suspect, from one of his oldest and dearest friends, who shall remain nameless.

MacDonald has a reputation for being loyal, kind, and giving to the women in his life; but true? He readily admits that he's not "lily-white," and that's not abnormal, when you consider that statistics state that more than 80 percent of the couples in this country cheat. MacDonald is simply in the majority, as is Randi.

After that of his family, Randi was, perhaps, at the time, MacDonald's biggest loss. She knew how to keep up with MacDonald's energy level. She knew how to handle the steady stream of women who kept trying to push their way into his life. Randi loved Jeff and she knew how to make him happy. This is a monumental feat because, as another ex-girlfriend, Susan, says, "Jeff is a very complex person." He can be totally dependable and predictable for a long period of time, and then simply withdraw from the scheme of whatever is going on at the moment with no explanation whatsoever. When confronted, his back goes up, and he gets furious that anyone would dare to question his actions--or lack of them.

Instead of asking straight-forward questions one must therefore manipulate the
answer in a round about way. Though one
of Jeff's pet hates is to be manipulated, he often leaves no alternative.

Susan is very attractive, bright and
nice. She holds one of the top career
jobs in the country, and unlike Mac-
Donald's other ex-girlfriends, she still
holds out hope that someday she will
marry him. MacDonald does not feel the
odds are promising, "There's simply too
much water over the dam," he says. For
the moment, they are good friends and
enjoy each other's company. Susan often
wishes she could forget MacDonald, but he
is not the kind of person one can forget
easily, if at all. In comtemplation of a
visit with MacDonald, after several
years' absence, Susan remarked that he
would soak her up like a wet sponge—and
she freely admits that this is exactly
what happened.

Whereas their friendship can be described as relatively tranquil, their
romance had some stormy moments, particularly at the end when MacDonald took
Susan out to dinner to tell her why it
was time for their romance to end. In
preparation for this traumatic occasion,
Susan shopped for the most exquisite out-
fit she could find, in hopes that their
romance would be rekindled. Instead, her
beautiful new blouse ended up with a
bucket full of tears, and MacDonald,
hating scenes of any kind, attempted to
cope with the situation as nearby

restaurant patrons took in Susan's tragedy sob by sob. Had MacDonald known what was in store for him that evening, he might have ended the romance sans the invitation to dinner.

The next day, Susan cleared her belongings out of MacDonald's condominium and scattered the gifts he had given her from one end of his living room to the other, knowing that if there's one thing that MacDonald cannot tolerate, it's disorder.

Susan has always given MacDonald the comfort of familiarity, but missing, during most of their relationship, was intrigue, at least on his part. A clue is her description of how he used to always read, rather than talk to her, even while they waited in line to buy tickets for a movie. Another indication occurred on a beach in Hawaii. Susan recalls trying to make conversation with MacDonald and being frustrated beyond comprehension when he finally told her (in his usual kind, gentle manner), to stop interrupting his train of thought and go call his mother (who was in Long Beach) and talk to her."

He complained to Susan about her feelings of insecurity toward him. However, it is clear to see that his popularity breeds insecurity into all but the most spirited. Insecure though she may feel, MacDonald has always been there when she needed him; in fact, he stayed at her father's side while he was dying, well after the romance had drawn its last breath.

Throughout the long years of struggle since they met, Susan and MacDonald have stayed in close touch, and it is likely they will remain devoted to each other.

The kind of woman MacDonald yearns for now would not likely be willing to put up with the constant advances of women from all over the country who, through widespread publicity, sympathize with MacDonald's troubles and want to help him. MacDonald does have an appeal that most women find irresistible.

He is flattered by their attentions and it is not easy for him to resist them. When those who know MacDonald well hear those Country and Western lyrics, "The angel in my arms this morning will be the devil in someone else's arms tonight," they can't help but think of him.

The new women who constantly come into his life run the full gamut. There are the pathetic who write hard-core porno fiction fantasies to him about the two of them together; or send marriage proposals in their first letter. Then come the lonely who cry out for his attention; the do-gooders, who sometimes do good but sometimes do more harm than good. The majority, however, are solid American citizens who are concerned about the injustices dealt him.

There are the high school and college students who write their term papers on the MacDonald case and often come up with evidence the defense has overlooked. There are hundreds of men and women of all ages who are kind, concerned and well-educated. They offer their help, their sympathy, and their friendship to MacDonald and for the most part, he welcomes it. This constant stream of attention, particularly from single women, would be unnerving to almost any girl. It led to the downfall of his romance with Susan, and it is likely to be a serious stumbling block with the attractive, strong, warm and loyal type woman MacDonald desires.

MacDonald's charisma makes him so much in demand by "other" women that past, present and predictable future incidents involving them, often makes the kind of woman who seriously appeals to MacDonald, leary of involvement with him.

Moreover, despite MacDonald's many brilliant and lovable qualities, the aftermath of the tragedies he has experienced has often led him to trust only those whom he can totally control.

Consequently, the kind of person who accepts this degree of control is often weak, insecure and unscrupulous, leading MacDonald into a vicious circle. The first time I visited MacDonald at the prison, we discussed his attitude about women. His conservative views and sensitive, protective feelings were a perfect match for the way he and his close friends described his treatment of Colette.

Soon after the visit, I met his mother. It was obvious to me from the

first moment we met that she was a great
lady, caring as deeply as one can about
the well-being of MacDonald and the rest
of her family. She was warm and cordial
and went out of her way to share some of
her knowledge about the personal side of
MacDonald's life with me.

When she said, "Jeff is quite taken
by you," I considered it the supreme
compliment--and it was. However, at that
time, I had no understanding of "The War
Among the Patriots," and, therefore, no
premonition of the double-edged sword
inherent in her statement.

As I became more involved in the
case, I began to help MacDonald co-
ordinate with the press and other people
with whom he dealt. Gradually, I began
to notice that MacDonald's mother seemed
wary of my growing involvement in the
case. Though she never said anything
specific, I felt that she suspected we
might be growing too close.

I relieved her mind of this notion
by explaining to her how crazy about my
husband and two children I am. I told her
of my five-year battle to win my husband;
and how there literally isn't a day of
the week that goes by that I don't think
to myself how lucky I am to have him and
our two mischievous nine and thirteen
year old boys. I believe she sensed I
was telling the truth and it kept our
friendship on an even keel for quite a
long period of time.

Rocky moments began again, however,
with the publishing of the "MacDonald

Newsletter." This publication has caused one of the larger battles in the "War Among the Patriots." "The MacDonald Newsletter" was conceived in November of 1984. It stemmed from a conversation between myself and MacDonald's private investigator, Ray Shedlick, about the need for a vehicle to get the true story of MacDonald and his case before the public. A positive newspaper or TV news segment here and there is not enough. To be convincing, no matter how truthful the news may be, there must be reinforcement if believability and confidence are to be established.

The "MacDonald Newsletter" appeared to fill a real need and seemed well-suited to this goal. It also pitted a few of MacDonald's old patriots against his new patriots, who were in whole responsible for publishing the newsletter. MacDonald's partner, Dr. Stephen Shea, and their secretary, Barbara Gallagher, had encountered bad experiences with the press. Their attitude, from what I can gather, is that the best way to deal with the case is to let the legal aspects of it stand on their own and to avoid publicity whenever possible.

Many of MacDonald's new friends believe that this stand is unrealistic. After all, the people in this country elect our government and they in turn appoint many of our judges. Our government and judges are human, just like the rest of us. They, too, have flaws, and for better or for worse, many cannot help being influenced by public opinion to some degree.

What most bothered the old patriots about the "MacDonald Newsletter" was the fact that though MacDonald had a strong say in its strategy, structure and content, they did not. MacDonald gave fair warning that there would be trouble, no matter how the newsletter turned out, and he was right. Fortunately, he waited as long as possible to break the news of its publication to his old patriots. Had they, the right hand, known what we, the left hand, were up to, it is highly likely that the first "MacDonald Newsletter" would never have gone to press.

The first issue brought forth two complaints: one, that it was too professional. The newsletter staff felt, however, that if it were to be taken seriously by the public, the press, the House of Representatives and the Senate, it must be professional, despite criticism that the "expensive look" would discourage donations to MacDonald's defense fund. We solved this dilemma by printing a disclaimer in subsequent issues, which stated that no funds for the newsletter would be taken from MacDonald's defense fund.

The other criticism involved a quote from MacDonald's daughter--"Daddy, Daddy, Daddy...why are they doing this to me?" The old patriots claimed it was sensationalism. In this instance, the new patriots agreed not to use any words that could in any way be twisted to translate

as sensationalism when discussing MacDonald's family. The exception is Mac-
Donald, who uses such phrases as, "the
slaughter of my family," and "brutally
murder Colette, Kim and Kristy," in the
"MacDonald Newsletter" with no criticism
from the old patriots whatsoever.

Later on, an extremely upsetting
discovery affected the credibility of
articles in several issues of the
"MacDonald Newsletter." This discovery
involved an alleged national organization of 12,000 members who befriended
MacDonald and offered to join the fight
for his freedom.

Their offer of help was gratefully
accepted by MacDonald, and he asked me to
meet with them, since we were within
commuting distance of each other. I felt
that inviting their "President" and "Secretary" (husband and wife) to join my
husband and me for dinner would be a nice
way to establish contact, and did so.

Though we didn't have much in common
with these people, they seemed pleasant
and I looked forward to working with
them. I should have been suspicious, however, when a national organization of
12,000 members could not spare enough
stamps to write letters in support of
MacDonald to various people, but I
wasn't. Like a fool, I went out and
bought stamps for them. At least I do believe they sent out some of the letters
for which I bought them stamps.

Again, I should have been suspicious
when this couple said they needed no

permission from members of their alleged
organization to publish excerpts from
their letters supporting MacDonald, in
the "MacDonald Newsletter." Unfortunately, I simply assumed that they knew
what they were doing. And, of course,
they did know what they were doing...I
didn't.

One of the most important things
they were supposedly working on was a
petition which was to be sent to the 4th
Circuit Court of Appeals to request a
hearing en banc should the court turn
down MacDonald's appeal. They bragged to
me, and no doubt to MacDonald, that they
had collected some 5,000-plus signatures.
I was thrilled, but I should have thought
something was amiss when the President
said it wouldn't be necessary for me to
pay the Federal Express bill to send the
petitions to the 4th Circuit Court after
MacDonald's appeal was turned down.
Instead, I was delighted that they finally had the money to pay for something,
and thought no more about it for quite
some time.

Early in 1986, I began to feel wary
of them, but I had no reason, and so kept
dismissing my feelings. Then one day
months later, my younger son asked me for
something from their organization to put
into his school report. It was then that
I realized that I had nothing. Why
didn't I have anything from this 12,000
member national organization?

Early the next morning, I awoke with
a start. Finally it came to me--there

was no national organization of 12,000
people. They had given me letters to
mail for other organizations of the same
kind they claimed to be, but never for
their own organization. Though there was
a time period when I saw them about once
a week, and talked to them almost daily,
I never met one member of their alleged
organization. I recall how, earlier this
year, they proudly told me that they had
again been elected President and Secretary of their organization, yet I never
thought to ask who, besides themselves,
elected them to their respective offices.

It was only about 4 a.m., but I
stumbled through the darkness, down the
hall, down the stairs, to the den where I
work on the case. I scrambled madly around, looking for evidence of the existence of their organization and found nothing. At 6 a.m. California time, I called the clerk at the 4th Circuit Court of
Appeals in Richmond, Virginia. I asked
if a petition had been filed in Mac-
Donald's behalf during the time of the
4th Circuit Court turn-down of Mac-
Donald's appeal.

The clerk read me the docket on the
case, and sure enough, there was no petition. I asked her to check through the
file of letters from the public. She said
that since petitions were considered
legaltype documents, it should have been
on the docket. Though she was familiar
with the case and had been with the court
a long time, she recalled no petition.
She said she would, however, check the

file of letters on the case from the public. She was gone for what seemed an eternity. When she finally returned, she said there was no petition in the files, no petition anywhere. I asked if they might have thrown it out. The clerk assured me this could not have happened. I couldn't believe it, but yet I could.

Next, I started calling groups that should have been familiar with the organization, in the towns where excerpts of letters from alleged supporters appeared in the "MacDonald Newsletter." Not one person from one organization in even the smallest town had ever heard of them. In fact, not even the Chamber of Commerce in their own small hometown had heard of them.

The President of this bogus 12,000 member national organization is into wars. He stated to my husband and me that he was fascinated by the Civil War and had fought in the Vietnam War. War, apparently, is one of his primary interests and sources of adventure in life. It must have been frustrating for him to come home from the Vietnam War and find himself a man without a war to fight.

MacDonald did not seem particularly surprised to find that this couple was living a lie and that their 12,000 member national organization was a non-existent fraud. Nor did MacDonald seem surprised that they had never filed their 5,000-plus signature petition with the 4th Circuit Court in support of his innocence.

After what McGinniss did to him,
MacDonald undoubtedly feels this is
relatively insignificant by comparison.
I, on the other hand, am not used to such
treatment. It was devastating to me to
discover that this couple had taken my
money, my time and my energy under fraudulent conditions. That time and time
again, they had lied to me. Lied to
MacDonald. Lied to MacDonald's supporters, and lied to the public. How tragic
that these two human beings felt the need
to stoop so low.

On the brighter side, in the third
issue of the newsletter, MacDonald's
partner, Dr. Stephen Shea, shared the
front page with MacDonald in an article
of support that was well-received by both
the old and new patriots.

The fourth newsletter brought forth
the first surprise criticism. It involved pictures of MacDonald's young
daughters, in a summary of the case which
he had written. It covered the time
period from just before the murders until
August '85. The old patriots claimed
that MacDonald's privacy had been invaded
by showing his new patriots pictures of
his family. However, MacDonald's mother
had, with his permission, given these and
numerous other family photographs to me,
to be used for whatever purpose was
deemed relevant and supportive of his
case.

The pictures were first used in his
hometown paper, "The Long Beach Press
Telegram." Knowing the pictures had

originally come from Mrs. MacDonald, a reporter from the paper called to verify who was in the pictures, where they were taken, and to obtain her permission to use them.

The next day, one of the pictures appeared in the paper, and there were numerous compliments about how well the picture showed the warmth of MacDonald's true character. Ironically, these pictures had been used in two national AP releases, as well as in many newspapers and TV news reports throughout the country prior to their publication in the "MacDonald Newsletter." There had been virtually no previous criticism, which makes it fairly obvious that the old patriots were showing their "possessive" traits; and, in an attempt to disguise them, implied that they were being protective of MacDonald's privacy.

Petty, insecure reactions such as these are human nature, and they are present in all of us. This kind of attitude is not just an example of war among MacDonald's patriots, but of the cause of everything from gang wars to world wars. The result replaces positive efforts and accomplishments with confusion and distraction.

It is important to understand here that if the new and the old patriots' positions were reversed, the new would, in all likelihood, react as do the old. In defense of the old patriots, it should be acknowledged that they have been loyal to MacDonald and supported him for a very long time. Some are tired now, and though the latest evidence is available for them to review, they simply don't. They know only that he's innocent, and they just want him out.

In addition to MacDonald's family, Dr. Shea and Barbara Gallagher have actually supported MacDonald on a daily basis since August, 1974, when the Justice Department reopened the case, until now. Dr. Shea has provided the majority of funds for MacDonald's defense. Barbara Gallagher mortgaged her house to help raise the money for his bail, while he was out on appeal during the latter part of 1980 through March of 1982. Clearly, a major part of their lives have been spent helping to free MacDonald. Without them, his chances for freedom might have been non-existent. Lawyers, private investigators, criminologists and witness expenses have been taken care of in large part by them. Their generosity is no doubt due to their strong belief in his innocence and their loyal devotion to him.

Despite bitter dissension between the old and the new, the "MacDonald Newsletter" survived and became stronger with each issue. In addition to MacDonald's supporters, about 525 members of the House and Senate receive it, and through national AP releases, major city newspapers, television and radio stations, hear about the newsletter and cover it with their audiences, making more and more people aware of the evidence and the fact that MacDonald has been railroaded and wrongfully convicted of the crimes.

In the beginning of my relationship with MacDonald, I had wondered why more of his friends didn't work together; but I soon took my place among the "new" and began to understand the "War Among the Patriots". I saw why secrecy on his part, in so many cases, was necessary for his survival.

When I met his secretary, Barbara Gallagher, one of the first things she said to me was, "I can't understand why I didn't hear about you before because Jeff tells me everything." At first I felt very unimportant, but I quickly came to know that Jeff MacDonald never tells anybody everything. Not Barbara, not his mother, not anyone...but he has a way of making the people close to him think they know everything. He is well aware, though, that the less he says, the less likely another battle in the "War Among the Patriots." On the other hand, MacDonald does confide in his patriots in areas that don't invite their individual envy. This way, all the patriots feel included and know that they are an important part of his life.

One senses MacDonald's dread of the least little confrontation, and after all he's been through, is easy to understand. MacDonald often avoids issues that he doesn't agree with, doesn't approve of, or hasn't made up his mind about, by simply remaining silent.

Until recently, it was a rarity when MacDonald wasn't cheerful; but it has become less rare lately, with the years of tragedy and anxiety finally beginning to take their toll.

With the passage of time, Dreyfus' patriots divided and tore each other apart, in all liklihood because Dreyfus was free and his cause was no longer a struggle that could blur rivalries and conceal fundamental differences.

With public support mounting for MacDonald, perhaps his troubles with the government will soon be over. The "War Among the Patriots," however, is as much about him as the cause involved, and is sure to go on as long as he does.

MACDONALD:
A PICTORIAL HISTORY

8

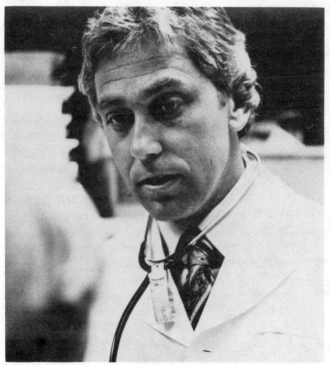

MacDonald practicing medicine at St. Mary Medical Center during the mid 1970's.

Above, Jeff Mac-
Donald as a baby.
having a bath in
the kitchen sink.
Below, Jeff taking
a walk in the
country.

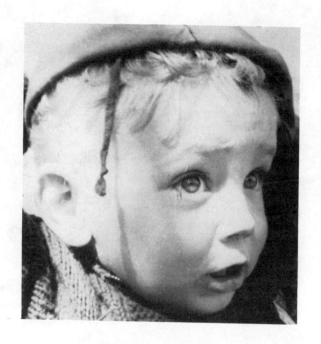

Jeff during his younger years.

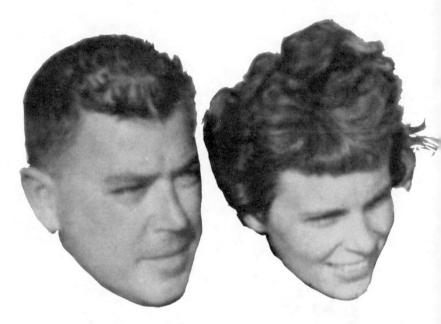

MacDonald's parents, James and Dorothy MacDonald.

Above, Jeff at the beach. Below, Jeff on his swing.

Above, Jeff at play.
Below, Jeff taking
a walk in the snow.

Above, MacDonald, right, fishing with his older brother, Jay. Below, MacDonald, right, with his older brother, Jay, on Long Island.

MacDonald during his teenage years.

**MacDonald's mother celebrating a
birthday during happier days.**

Colette and Jeff at their wedding reception,
September, 1963.

Colette and Jeff with members of
the wedding party.

MacDonald in his Green Beret uniform.

MacDonald with his daughters.

MacDonald playing with his daughters.

Kimberly with her teddy bear. Below, Kimberly reading her storybook.

Above, Kimberly watching over Kristin.
Below, Kimberly and Kristin dressed up
for Halloween.

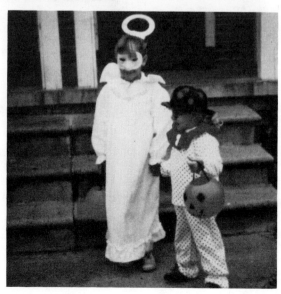

MacDonald in front of Court House during 1979 trial in Raleigh, North Carolina.

Above, Brian O'Neill,
Chief Counsel for
1984-85 evidentiary hear-
ings and 1985 Appeal,
4th Circuit Court.
Below, Bernard Segal,
Chief Counsel for 1979
trial and appeals follow-
ing the trial.

Above,
Ray Shedlick,
MacDonald's Chief
Investigator, post-
trial to present.
Below, Ray
Shedlick's
daughter, Ellen,
who worked closely
on the case with
her father.

MacDonald's sister, Judy Alvey; niece Samantha Alvey, and friend Kathy Gillis mailing an issue of the "MacDonald Newsletter."

Left to right: Dennis Eisman, Melinda Stephens, Mrs. Ray Shedlick and Ray Shedlick, at the Richmond, Virginia, airport.

MacDonald at FCI-Bastrop

FCI-Bastrop, foreground, weight-lifting equipment; background, factory where helmets and lifeboat covers are manufactured.

FCI-Bastrop, foreground, weight-lifting equipment and baseball field.

202

FCI-Bastrop cafeteria.

FCI-Bastrop General Library.

FCI-Bastrop Graphic Arts Center.

FCI-Bastrop Machine Shop.

MacDonald in front of his dorm at FCI-Bastrop.

MacDonald at FCI Bastrop.

MacDonald

MacDonald at FCI-Phoenix.

FCI-Phoenix.

MacDonald.

MACDONALD'S KITCHEN CABINET

9

If there's one thing MacDonald's Kitchen Cabinet has in common with Reagan's Kitchen Cabinet it's "politics." There are the mad scrambles for progress and power, precarious juggling acts to keep afloat, and the cloak and dagger hysteria inherent in this pursuit.

There is no doubt that life as a member of MacDonald's Kitchen Cabinet can be very difficult for those who believe in his innocence. (As opposed to "adventurists" who came on-board for thrills.) It is also rewarding, because there is the opportunity to help a man who is a joy to know for his perceptive intelligence, wit and sensitivity...and an honor to know for his commitment to humanity in the field of medicine.

MacDonald's kitchen cabinet is headed by MacDonald and, until the fall of '86, his defense attorney of record, Brian O'Neill. O'Neill was the former Chief of Special Prosecutions for the U.S. Attorney's office in Los Angeles.

He also was affiliated with the prestigious law firm headed by former National Democratic Committee Chairman, Charles Mannat. O'Neill now heads his own law firm located in Santa Monica, California. O'Neill is smart, so smart, that in fact, it's often difficult to keep up with his thought process, despite being thoroughly knowledgeable about the subject at hand. O'Neill is exceptionally well-liked in political circles because he is honest and he is not a "back stabber." Andrea VandeKamp, whose husband, John, ran against O'Neill for Attorney General of California (and won), states that Brian O'Neill is the nicest man she has ever met. Perhaps this letter from O'Neill to MacDonald best illustrates her point.

December 23, 1982

Dear Jeff:

Best wishes for the best Christmas possible under the circumstances. I want you to know that while you are alone physically, you are not alone spiritually. Your friends, who are really an extended family, are with you practically 24 hours a day and will remain so. We all are constantly reminded by the incredible loyalty and affection expressed by your friends and colleagues how much you mean to them. Their support of you, reflected by their almost daily requests to be of assistance, is more than most people receive in their life.

None of that removes you from your present situation, but all of it is important in working toward that end.

I don't have it at hand, and can't even come close to quoting it, but the Irish poet, Yeats, wrote about the greatest light and greatest opportunities emerging from the darkest pits. That is more than Irish sentimentality. It is our collective experience.

We are going to get out of that dark pit and correct this wrong, and we're going to do it because of the support, encouragement and assistance of all your many friends. Believe me, they remain your friends, and they remain intensely loyal.

Merry Christmas,
Brian

    I first met Brian O'Neill in late December of 1983. MacDonald had sent me to him for approval on an article I wanted to write about him shortly after he had been devastated by McGinniss' "Fatal Vision." O'Neill makes an awe-inspiring first impression. His quiet yet friendly personality exudes a confidence that is compatible with his absolutely perfect features, highlighted by piercing yet gentle brown eyes, and a handsome, well-built body.

We discussed the case, what Mac-
Donald has been through and his hopes toward MacDonald's vindication. At the conclusion of our meeting, O'Neill gave me
the go-ahead to visit MacDonald and write
the article, providing MacDonald agreed,
which he did.

When O'Neill came on board in September, 1982, he walked into total political dissention among the Kitchen Cabinet. In all honesty, this dissention was
and is a very common happening both in
MacDonald's case and in the Dreyfus case,
and in each, became a rampant despoiler
of hearts and minds. There had been
massive complaints since MacDonald's 1979
trial, from the ranks on up, about his
previous lawyer, Bernard Segal. Segal
had been brilliant at the Article 32
Hearing which exonerated MacDonald.

Segal utilized artist conception
drawings rendered shortly after the
crime, of three of the people MacDonald
described as having attacked him. These
people were discovered to have been in
the same drug cult, and were seen in
close vicinity of the MacDonald home by
other witnesses at the time the crimes
were committed. Since this time, two of
the three people MacDonald described have
confessed.

Segal also relied upon expert
psychiatric testimony. The defense psychiatrist said that MacDonald was incap-
able of committing a crime of this
magnitude, and the government psychiatrist from Walter Reed Army Hospital

said that had MacDonald committed a crime
of this magnitude, he would have lost his
mind, which he has not done, not even in
the most temporary sense.

Segal also proved that the physical
evidence was inconsistent with MacDonald
having committed the crimes, as discussed
in Chapter 3 in the section reviewing the
45 items indicating intruders had been
present in the MacDonald home, as well as
other sections in that chapter.

Segal, however, did not fare so well
at MacDonald's 1979 civilian trial. Many
believed that Segal's aggressive
personality, flamboyant courtroom manner,
combined with his being Jewish and from
California did not bode well, and, in
fact, was a disaster in the deeply southern, staunchly conservative City of Raleigh, North Carolina. Here, it is unlikely that a black or Jew has ever been
a member of the Tennis Club where Judge
Dupree spent much of his time. The
Tennis Club may be more liberal now, but
Judge Dupree clearly remains as he was in
1979.

After the jury convicted MacDonald,
Segal took the case to the 4th Circuit
Court of Appeals, where MacDonald's guilty verdict was overturned and MacDonald
went free on bail. After the Supreme
Court overturned the 4th Circuit Court
verdict and MacDonald was returned to
prison, the Segal/MacDonald relationship
went steadily downhill and MacDonald
began to look seriously at other lawyers.
He and those in the cabinet felt that

characteristics the opposite of Segal's were in order, particularly since a new trial might well take place in Raleigh, North Carolina.

Brian O'Neill fit the bill to perfection. O'Neill, experienced, wise in the world of politics, and an excellent judge of character, complemented MacDonald's weakest areas of expertise. He was one of the first, if not "the" first, to predict that Joe McGinniss might not be writing a favorable book about MacDonald.

One of the first changes O'Neill made was to replace Ted Gunderson as the private investigator in MacDonald's case. Gunderson was the former special agent in charge of the Western region of the FBI. He, along with former police officer, Prince Beasley, was the first to reinvestigate the case after MacDonald's 1979 trial. At the time the crimes took place, Prince Beasley had recognized Helena Stoeckley as fitting the description MacDonald had given of one of his attackers. He, along with Gunderson, again found Stoeckley and obtained a signed confession of her presence and involvement in the murders.

The problem O'Neill had with Gunderson was the same that Segal had, and stemmed from the fact that Gunderson was not always a team player. After much of the new evidence had been gathered, despite clear orders to keep it under wraps, Gunderson turned it all over to the FBI. This meant that the government had an opportunity to threaten the confessors, one of whom died of mysterious causes shortly thereafter. The government also had an opportunity to attempt, through innuendo, to discredit physical evidence as well as the expert witnesses who were ready to corroborate this testimony. Many believe that had the government been taken by surprise with all the evidence at the time of the evidentiary hearings, that MacDonald would now be a free man. We'll never know.

O'Neill hired a former New York City detective, Raymond Shedlick, to take over Gunderson's responsibilities. Shedlick opened an office in Durham, North Carolina, for the primary purpose of investigating the MacDonald case. Tall and pleasant looking, Shedlick comes across as an honest and gentle man. He is personable and down to earth, capable of getting along with everyone from the most humble and/or difficult, to the President of the United States. His warmth and kindness combined with a lively sense of humor, gave witnesses who had been afraid to talk for years, the confidence to tell what they knew about the crimes.

I met Ray Shedlick for the first time during the evidentiary hearings. There were two sessions, with the last session having been scheduled for a summation of the arguments. In preparation for this last session, Murphy's law prevailed. Myrna Greenberg, a lawyer who worked for Brian O'Neill on the

MacDonald case, asked me if I knew an artist who could draw up charts listing each of the confessors and the witnesses who corroborated the confessor's statements, as well as a map of the area where the murders took place. I gave Myrna the name of Glenda Fowler, an artist who also donates time to the "MacDonald Newsletter."

O'Neill & Company were very pleased with Glenda's work; however, with the last minute additions they made, there was no way the charts and map could be ready when O'Neill and Greenberg were scheduled to leave for Raleigh, North Carolina, where the hearings took place. Since I was scheduled to leave about 14 hours later, it was decided that I would take the charts and the map. In addition, David Yarnell, a producer who supports MacDonald's innocence, was combining the audio and video portions of the confession Helena Stoeckley had made for "60 Minutes" so that it could be entered into the court records. There were all kinds of unforeseen technical problems which came up, and despite round-the-clock efforts, the tape was not ready before MacDonald's lawyers departed. Therefore, I was also elected to take Helena Stoeckley's taped confession to Raleigh.

I was to leave on an 11 p.m. flight to Raleigh and things started going wrong from the moment I got up that morning. 100 mph winds had cut off the electricity which added up to starting the day with no coffee--nothing compared to the news Glenda's phone call brought. Glenda called around 10:00 a.m. to say that the roof had blown off her house and that she was afraid that the charts and the map had blown away. Despite her personal disaster, I begged her to do everything. she could to find them because, in a sense, a man's life was at stake. She promised she would.

In the meantime, David Yarnell arrived with the tape--the first thing to go right all morning. When I told David about the charts and the map, he suggested that I forewarn Brian and Myrna. I decided not to, however, because they wouldn't arrive in Raleigh to get the message until about 10:00 p.m. that night, at which time there would be nothing they could do about it. Besides that fact, I still held out a glimmer of hope that Glenda would find the charts and the map, in which case there would be no point in worrying them.

By the time I finished with necessary family errands and arrived back home, it was getting dark--and still no electricity, no maps and no charts. I began to pack in the dark with a flashlight. Not wanting to be alone in the dark, my two young boys followed me everywhere, constantly asking when their father, who had gone out to get us all pizza, would be home. When it was almost time to go to the airport, there was a loud knock on the door and when I opened it, there stood Glenda's son with the charts. Things began to look up again, though the map was apparently lost forever. Just before I left for the airport, Jeff's Mom called to see how things were going. When I told her what had happened she said how typical it was in her son's case to never have anything run smoothly. She was relieved to know that just about everything had been salvaged, and wished me a safe trip.

Another problem developed when I took the charts aboard the Delta flight to Raleigh. They would not fit in the overhead rack or under the seat. In fact, they seemingly would not fit anywhere, and I refused to allow them to travel in the baggage compartment, because if they went on to another city, it might be impossible to retrieve them in time for the hearing. Finally, after explaining the seriousness of their potential loss, the cabin attendant spoke with the Captain who found a place for the charts in the cockpit. By the time the plane finally landed in Raleigh, I looked like something the cat dragged in.

On the one hand, I hoped that Ray Shedlick, who had planned to meet my plane unless an emergency came up, wouldn't be there to see me looking so bedraggled. On the other hand, I realized that if he didn't meet me, it would be almost impossible to carry everything. He was there, and we went directly to the hotel where we met Brian O'Neill and Myrna Greenberg for breakfast. I informed Brian, who had the flu, that Glenda's roof had blown off and although the charts had been salvaged, the map was lost. I'm not sure whether he believed this incredibly far-fetched story then, but if he didn't, he did when he got back home after the hearings and found the story about Glenda's roof on the front page of the paper.

Back in Raleigh, the evidentiary hearings went smoothly, if not justly. One of the toughest things for Shedlick, as well as many other MacDonald supporters to understand, was that unfortunately "southern justice" still prevails in some instances in the South. Shedlick was shocked when Judge Dupree refused to recuse himself from the case because his son-in-law had been one of MacDonald's chief prosecutors. He was even more shocked when a newspaper article came out during the evidentiary hearings, quoting Judge Dupree's former son-in-law, as still being very much involved in the case. This article was the basis for the defense's second request that Judge Dupree recuse himself; yet he refused again, stating that he had never discussed the case with his former son-in-law. Shedlick knew differently however. In fact, he knew they were working to some extent on the case together, because he had seen Jimmy Proctor in the Federal Courthouse arranging for a Federal Express package to be delivered to Judge Dupree's chambers during the evidentiary hearings.

This indiscretion makes it clear

that Judge Dupree lied all along about his involvement with his son-in-law. From that point forward, Shedlick probably realized that whether he produced 35 witnesses or 3,500 witnesses who corroborated the confessors to the crimes, Dupree would in all probability ignore them all; not to mention the physical evidence favorable to the defense. The hopelessness of the situation no doubt depressed Shedlick, and defense funds to pay him ran out shortly after the evidentiary hearings.

Shedlick, however, remains on the case to this day and bills MacDonald only for his expenses. Shedlick also handles investigative responsibilities for the civil suit MacDonald has filed against "Fatal Vision" author Joe McGinniss. On this case, he reports to civil attorney, Gary Bostwick.

Big and broad shouldered with piercing brown eyes, Bostwick gives the appearance of someone you wouldn't want to cross swords with. He is a clever man with an especially difficult task, because of the fact that MacDonald stands convicted of the murders of his family.

Dennis Eisman, a Philadelphia defense attorney who had assisted Bernard Segal during the Article 32 Hearing, helped bolster both the civil and the defense case in 1984 by publishing an article about the injustices dealt Mac-Donald in the Philadelphia Law Review's "Shingle" magazine. The article served to lift MacDonald's spirits considerably and created renewed interest in both the civil and defense cases among defense attorneys and prosecutors alike.

After Judge Dupree turned down MacDonald's request for a new trial in a 110 page decision which ignored all 35 new witnesses and the government suppressed physical evidence, Brian O'Neill prepared to take the case to the 4th Circuit Court of Appeals. Due in large part to the damage "Fatal Vision" had done both in regard to the case and MacDonald's image, it was decided that an Amicus Curiae (friend of the Court brief) would be a valuable tool in adding strength to the true facts of the case.

Eisman came through with the support of the National Association of Criminal Defense Lawyers, an organization of close to 5,000 of the top defense lawyers in the country. Eisman wrote the brief, which followed closely along the lines of O'Neill's brief (as is required by law), and there were high hopes that this would serve the purpose for which it was created. Oral arguments took place in Richmond, Virginia, on October 7, 1985. It was the first time that many on MacDonald's defense team had an opportunity to meet in person.

With the exception of Mike Malley and Brian O'Neill, MacDonald's defense team stayed at the John Marshall Hotel. This hotel is within walking distance of the Courthouse and though no longer the most modern of those available, it has become a tradition for lawyers and clients in town for court proceedings to stay there. Almost without exception, both the prosecution and defense for each appeal in this 16-year case have stayed there, and this occasion was no different.

Dr. Jane DiGiovanni and her husband, Dr. Stephen Smith, were the first to arrive. They have done extensive research into the government's infamous footprint theory and found, that literally speaking, it didn't have a leg to stand on. There was in fact not one piece of concrete evidence that indicated the foot print belonged to MacDonald.

Eileen Foster, a Houston NBC News producer and I arrived next. Then came Ray Shedlick and his wife, along with Denny Eisman, followed later on by Rick Towne, a civil attorney who assisted Gary Bostwick in the fraud suit against McGinniss. All accept Towne met early in the evening for cocktails and dinner at the hotel's restaurant. As the luck of the draw would have it, we were seated next to the prosecution. Included at their table were Brian Murtagh, John DePue (an assistant U.S. Attorney), Fred Kassab, and retired CID agent Peter Kearns. Mildred Kassab was not present and there are rumors that she is seriously ill...of what, I haven't heard. One of the members of the defense team suggested that we move to another table, but I said, "Lets's stay, let them move."

I don't think they heard me, but they did move.

Though it was the defense team's first time together, we had all talked with each other at length on the phone and there had been endless correspondence between us, so everything was very relaxed and amicable. After dinner, Drs. DiGiovanni and Smith headed for the bar for a nightcap. As the rest of us left to go to our various rooms, Rick Towne arrived and knowing him better than the others did, I kept him company while he had dinner. As Rick's first course was cleared away and the main course served, voices from the direction of the bar began to get louder and louder.

Finally, Rick said something to the effect of, "My God, what's going on in there?" I explained that Drs. DiGiovanni and Smith were having a discussion about the MacDonald case with Peter Kearns and his wife and that the voices he heard were predominantly those of Peter Kearns and his wife. Towne expressed surprise at this spontaneous defense/prosecution hearing of the case taking place at the bar of a public hotel. I assured him one took place at that very bar every time there was a new appeal on the case. From then on, if anything surprised him, he didn't let on and simply took it in stride.

The next morning we all gathered in the courtroom. We stood up as the four judges hearing the oral argument for MacDonald's appeal took their places. I had immediate misgivings because they looked so stone-faced and bored--without

concern or feelings. I wondered if they
had seriously considered the brief with
all of its accompanying documents, and if
they were going to listen to the
arguments or nap until the arguments were
over and it was time for lunch. They
didn't go to sleep, but they didn't
express much interest in the case either.
Though it was undetectable in the courtroom, there was dissention between
O'Neill and Eisman. Only 30 minutes was
allowed for each side to speak. Eisman
had requested a portion of this time to
speak in support of his Amicus Curiae
brief, but O'Neill, as MacDonald's
Attorney of Record, held firm in using
all the time. He said it was little
enough to summarize a 16 year case.

Another concern O'Neill had in
allowing Eisman to speak was an error in
Eisman's Amicus brief which stated that
Judge Dupree had refused to grant
MacDonald an Evidentiary Hearing. Though
Eisman had requested the Court to strike
that comment from the record, O'Neill was
afraid the Judges might use up valuable
time discussing this error, leaving him
less time to argue the evidence in
support of a new trial for MacDonald.

Some of the key MacDonald supporters
felt that Eisman was a more persuasive
speaker than O'Neill. At the beginning
of each MacDonald court proceeding,
O'Neill did begin with a hesitant, "stage
fright" like quality which disappeared
after the first five or ten minutes,
after which his arguments built to a

riveting crescendo that several times left prosecutor Brian Murtaugh red-faced and stuttering. O'Neill's ending remarks at the oral arguments in Richmond prompted one of MacDonald's closest friends, Ray Shea to tell MacDonald that he was so moved by O'Neill's statements that he felt like standing up and cheering.

After the hearing adjourned, we all went back to the hotel for lunch. I went up to my room to call the operator to tell her that should MacDonald call any of us, to transfer our calls to the dining room. I barely got the words out of my mouth when she said, "Don't you dare move from that room. Dr. Mac-Donald's been calling you every few minutes and he'll be calling again any minute." I obeyed her and sat down on the bed making notes about the hearing while I waited for his call. It came, not more than a minute later. After giving MacDonald a blow by blow description of the argument, I gave him a list of the press who wanted to speak with him. He agreed to call back in a half hour to find out what arrangements I could make with them in regard to time, deadlines, etc. By the time I got to the dining room, everyone in our party had left. As I got off the elevator to go back to my room I found Ray Shedlick, who had just missed a call from MacDonald, scurrying to Eileen Foster's room to try to catch him there. I told Shedlick that if he missed him that he would be calling me again shortly.

While awaiting MacDonald's next call, I ordered lunch from room service, and seconds after putting the receiver down, there was a knock on the door. Upon opening it, I found the entire MacDonald crew there, with the exception of Brian O'Neill and Mike Malley. They had all missed his call and decided to try to speak to him from my room, which they did. MacDonald called as scheduled, and after giving him a list of whom to call when, everyone else got on the phone one by one with his/her version of the oral arguments. While this was going on, my lunch came. The two chairs in my single room were filled, people sat on my bed and sat on the floor. In essence, the scene was wall to wall people. The perplexed waiter asked where to put my lunch and, after surveying the scene, I told him to put it in the closet. He understandably looked at me as if I had lost my mind, but it was the best, in fact only, place to put it.

In less than an hour it was time to pack up and leave Richmond. Drs. Smith and DiGiovanni, Denny Eisman, Ray Shedlick and his wife and I gathered at the airport for what would be the last friendly get together before another bout of dissension maimed the Kitchen Cabinet. We discussed MacDonald's chances for a positive 4th Circuit decision. We were all relieved (though in retrospect, wrongly so) that Judge Murgnahan was one of the three judges to hear the case.

The reasoning here was that although MacDonald's last appeal, based on Due Process of Law, had been turned down, Judge Murgnahan had stated in one decision that "Given the wide discretion vested in the trial judge, we should not fault Judge Dupree to the extent of reversing. Nevertheless, in view of the issues involved, and the virtually unique aspects of the surrounding circumstances, had I been the trial judge, I would have exercised the wide discretion conferred on him to allow the testimony to come in. My preference derives from my belief that, if the jury may be trusted with ultimate resolution of factual issues, it should not be denied the opportunity of obtaining a rounded picture necessary for resolution of the large questions, by withholding of collateral testimony consistent with and basic to the defendant's principal exculpatory contention. If such evidence were not persuasive, which is what the government essentially contends in saying that it was untrustworthy, the jury, with very great probability, would not have been misled by it."

Our hopes however, were mingled with a sense of foreboding because Murgnahan stated during this round: "I have already expressed myself as regarding the Stoeckley information that wasn't introduced, and I think we're probably beyond the time that anything can be done about it, but it's been troubling to me because if the Government's position was right that nobody would believe Ms. Stoeckley, why were they afraid of the jury, why didn't they let the jury decide?

"If, on the other hand, he--she would have, perhaps, created some reasonable doubt on the part of the jury, I'm-- I regret, still regret, although I think it's all over..."

At this point my flight to Washington, D.C., was called and I left to keep my appointment with congressman Glenn Anderson's staff. After a successful meeting, Congressman Anderson supported MacDonald as per excerpts from this news story, which follows:

Rep. Anderson requests new trial for MacDonald

'Due process may have been denied'

By Larry Keller
Staff writer

Former St. Mary Medical Center doctor and convicted murderer Jeffrey MacDonald should be given a new trial in order to determine the facts in his case, Rep. Glenn Anderson, D-Long Beach said in a prepared statement released Wednesday.

Anderson said that he is concerned about "a number of instances where due process may have been denied" in the case of the former Army captain.

"I understand seven witnesses who corroborate the account of gang involvement (in the murders of MacDonald's wife and two daughters) were not allowed to testify at his (1979) trial, and now over 30 more witnesses have come forward," stated Anderson in the release.

While stopping short of saying that MacDonald is innocent, Anderson did praise him as "one of the founders of our country's trauma and paramedic system," and noted that he is "well-respected" by local police and a lifetime honorary member of the Long Beach Police Officers Association.

MacDonald came to Long Beach in 1970 as an emergency-

room physician at St. Mary's, and was later promoted to head of the unit.

Anderson said that in September he wrote Attorney General Edwin Meese asking if he had appointed a special prosecutor to review the case, or taken any other action that might result in a new trial for MacDonald.

The congressman said he was informed that the Department of Justice "knows of absolutely no grounds" to support the appointment of a special prosecutor.

Because of controversy in the MacDonald case, "it seems that a new trial would be in order to determine the facts by examining all the evidence available," said Anderson in the statement. "That seems the least we can do to ensure justice in this case."

MacDonald was convicted by a federal court jury in Raleigh, N.C., in 1979 of fatally stabbing and bludgeoning his pregnant wife, Collette, 26, and his daughters, Kimberly, 5, and Kristen, 2. The slayings occurred at Fort Bragg, N.C., in 1970.

MacDonald, who has insisted the murders were committed by a band of drug-crazed hippies, is serving three consecutive life sentences at the federal penitentiary in Bastrop, Tex.

The doctor was originally cleared of the murders by an Army panel, but the case has been in and out of the courts for

New trial for MacDonald urged

10 years. The case became the subject of the best-selling book, "Fatal Vision," which was subsequently made into a television mini-series.

The concerns raised by Anderson mirror those raised by MacDonald's attorneys and supporters. One of the latter, Melinda Stephens, said she met with Bob Freeland, the congressman's administrative assistant, in October to lobby for support. She also left material with him outlining the case for MacDonald's innocence.

Stephens writes a monthly newsletter that is mailed to MacDonald supporters and elected officials. She said Anderson's comments would be included in the next issue, as will excerpts from a new book by former Los Angeles County Coroner Thomas Noguchi, who questions some of the findings in the MacDonald case.

Anderson could not be reached for comment. But Freeland said his boss got involved in the case because of MacDonald's Long Beach background and the esteem in which he is held by the police officers' association.

I then went to visit MacDonald at Bastrop, Texas. We discussed his case and we talked about MacDonald's mother, and his concern about her health. MacDonald was understandably tired that day. Tired of the case. Tired of the fight and frustrated at the seeming inability of justice to prevail. I left to fly home with a continued sense of foreboding about the 4th Circuit Court Decision.

As MacDonald, his family, friends and defense team waited, a rumor quickly spread about a book authored by Dr. Thomas Noguchi, entitled "Coroner at Large," which discussed the MacDonald case. After finding that the book was not yet available in bookstores, I called the publisher, who put me in touch with Dr. Noguchi's publicist, Jennifer Kittridge. Ms. Kittridge told me that they had been trying to locate MacDonald to send him copies of the book. She sent both of us copies via overnight courier and we were ecstatic to find there was a whole chapter on the MacDonald case with numerous positive statements and useful insights.

Most importantly, the chapter stated that the CID bloodtyping, one of the major factors which convicted MacDonald at his 1979 trial, was different from the FBI's bloodtyping, and that this had never been revealed to MacDonald's defense. In addition, Noguchi stated that he could not understand how the same forensic evidence that exonerated MacDonald at the Article 32 Hearings could convict him at his 1979 trial. Noguchi's book clearly stated that whether guilty or innocent, MacDonald did not receive a fair trial.

Dr. Noguchi's co-author, Joe DiMona called me several days later to offer help on the case and suggested that a telephone call be arranged between Noguchi and MacDonald. At his suggestion and that of Jennifer Kittridge, I telephoned Dr. Noguchi, who was willing to speak with MacDonald and to see what he could

do to help. They had a positive conversation, and arrangements for a meeting
with MacDonald's lawyer and Noguchi's
lawyer were made. Shortly thereafter,
Noguchi agreed to examine the forensics
in the MacDonald case to see whether he
could come up with newly discovered
evidence which would powerfully support
MacDonald's innocence.

Dr. Noguchi stated that he would
base his findings strictly on autopsy
material, because he believes the results
are incontestable. After his review,
Dr.Noguchi declared Dr. MacDonald unquestionably innocent.

It was a time full of high hopes
when, on December 17, 1985, a negative
decision from the 4th Circuit Court
landed with a thud. When MacDonald
called to tell me the news, I was taken
totally by surprise, as was he, when his
lawyer had called him. It was hard to
believe such a cruel decision could be
reached just before Christmas. The next
day I assured MacDonald that everyone I
had spoken with was still behind him and
that we would fight on for him with more
determination than ever before.

MacDonald's lawyer, Brian O'Neill,
requested that the 4th Circuit Court hear
the case en banc, which means that
instead of three judges hearing the case,
all 12 judges would re-hear the case.

In the meantime, just two days after
the 3-judge decision, MacDonald was
transferred, with no notice, and only the
clothes on his back, to a prison in

Phoenix, Arizona. Two shocks in one week
were almost too much to bear for those of
us close to him. Ironically, he seemed
to bear up best of all, with the kind of
determined strength that has kept him
going through all of these painful years.

In January, 1986, MacDonald's en
banc hearing was turned down and we began
to create a campaign to educate the
public about the evidence supporting his
innocence. "Fatal Vision" had taken its
toll, and without the public knowing and
understanding the truth, there would be
no hope for MacDonald to receive a
Presidential pardon should the Supreme
Court refuse to hear the case.

As Brian O'Neill prepared a brief
for the Supreme Court, so did Dennis
Eisman. MacDonald was frustrated that
Brian O'Neill didn't get him a rough of
the brief early on so that he would have
plenty of time to give O'Neill his input.
Though O'Neill has a history of
presenting accurate, well thought out and
all-in-all outstanding briefs, MacDonald
became increasingly upset when he still
had seen only a partially completed rough
brief just two weeks before it was to be
filed with the Supreme Court.

Worse, when O'Neill's complete brief
finally did arrive at the prison, it was
delivered to MacDonald a day late. In
the meantime, MacDonald had allowed Eisman to "railroad" him into accepting his
brief rather than O'Neill's. Several
weeks prior to this decision, Eisman had
gone to visit MacDonald in Phoenix and

catered to his every whim. Eisman put into his brief just about whatever MacDonald requested. Then he convinced MacDonald that it should be printed and filed with the Supreme Court several days before the deadline. MacDonald had always been understandably nervous about filing briefs right at the deadline, and therefore, the early printing and early filing greatly appealed to him. On the other hand, it is common practice among a number of highly thought of attorneys to file at the last second because they are driven to "give it all they've got."

Many people feel that what Eisman did was highly unethical. Whatever the pros and cons, he unduly pressured MacDonald to file early. He then avoided Brian O'Neill when at the last minute, after MacDonald ordered O'Neill to stop Eisman. Instead, Eisman dashed up the Supreme Court steps to file the brief.

This incident has caused a tremendous split in the cabinet. Eisman has told MacDonald that he wants to take over his entire case, and in October of '86 he did take over MacDonald's defense case. Some see him as an opportunist and feel that had he taken on other aspects of the case, thereby joining a team effort, MacDonald's chances with the Supreme Court would have been far greater. Certain of those who have seen O'Neill's Supreme Court Brief state that it is clearly more focused on key issues than is Eisman's brief. On the other hand, there are those who have raved about

Eisman's brief. Others feel that Eisman
has more energy and is more aggressive
than O'Neill and should take over the
case.

MacDonald, of course, suffers the
most from the "politics" involved in situations such as this one.

Since the cabinet split, well-
meaning but embarrassingly unqualified
people have made a fool of MacDonald both
with his supporters and in public.
Strikingly and disturbingly similar to
these incompetents were those involved in
the Dreyfus case, who are described as
people with neither a past of appropriate
education and culture, nor current
training to destine them for the work at
hand--with their biggest dilemma being to
decipher which way the wind is blowing in
time to shift their course.

If Eisman is not strong enough to
insist that these people desist and
well-qualified professionals take over,
MacDonald will suffer immeasurably. If
Eisman is successful in this endeavor,
then I believe all who accuse him of
opportunism must ignore their personal
feelings of the past and place their support behind him. If Eisman fails in this
endeavor, MacDonald is clearly in need of
new legal counsel.

Disagreements among the Kitchen Cabinet and the mad scrambles for power
which accompany them, often take on more
importance than the case itself and could
be responsible for MacDonald losing the
freedom he has fought so long and hard to

regain.

LIFE ON THE OTHER SIDE OF THE FENCE

10

Being the only American in a Chinese jail can have its advantages tourist Richard S. Ondrik said. The warden in the Harbin, China jail made dumplings for him, and a trustee hauled hot water for his weekly bath. But despite the decent treatment, Ondrik states, " a cage is a cage no matter how golden."

The razor wire fence at The Federal Correctional Institute at Bastrop, Texas, does not look particularly menacing to me...but then, my hands have never been cut by razor wire. The guards at FCI-Bastrop will tell you that the rocks on the "freedom" side of the fence are wired and should they be stepped on an alarm will go off. This may be true, but I doubt it, and I'll tell you why. One day when MacDonald and I were sitting in the visiting room, the guard (often referred to as "the hack") said "All right, that's it you two, visit's over". Knowing that we hadn't done anything wrong, I looked in back of me and saw a man, who looked more like a boy of about 19, with his arm around a girl who looked even younger. It seems they had broken the head warden's cardinal rule with regard to affection, a rule which states that each inmate and his visitor are allowed one kiss upon entering the visiting room and one kiss upon leaving the visiting room.

The outcome of this particular situation was that she was escorted out of the visiting room and he was escorted to solitary confinement, more commonly referred to as "the hole". MacDonald told me that this couple was almost always in some sort of trouble and that the man had just recently been released from the hole, after an untimely visit with his girlfriend at the razor wire fence. It seems that she had ridden her horse up to the fence in anticipation of an unauthorized visit. Though the horse trampled all over the rocks, the alarm never went off, and that's why I don't think there's anything under those rocks except maybe a cantankerous old rattlesnake or two.

Though there are no cells and I haven't seen any bars, security is tight at FCI-Bastrop. The residents live in modern dorm-like structures in small rooms that contain bed and bath facilities as well as a desk. The only necessity missing is a shower which must be taken elsewhere in the "dorm". There is also a small recreation area in the dorm with food and drink machines and pay telephones.

If you have to be locked up, however, there are better places to be, such as the numerous prisons throughout the country with individual pay telephones and television sets in each room. And of course there are worse places to be; like Leavenworth, a maximum security prison in Kansas, where some of the country's most violent prisoners are housed. Unlike Bastrop, Leavenworth has the ugly gray forbidding walls, filth, and squalor one so often sees depicted at the movies or on television.

Perhaps the most terrifying prison experience anyone has suffered was that of Dreyfus at Devil's Island. Here Dreyfus, for all intents and purposes lived in a cage where he could not sleep because insects ran over his skin and the heat often reached 104o. Worse, much of Dreyfus' time was spent shackled to an iron bed inside his cage. Letters from his children and his faith that he would eventually be reunited with his family, he states, gave him the will to survive. One letter says, "Dearest Papa...I would like you to come back soon. You must ask the good Lord. As for me, I ask him every day...Many kisses. Your little Jeanne." A letter from Dreyfus' son Pierre states: "Dearest Papa, I cried this morning because you are not coming back, and it causes me too much pain..."

Though Dreyfus suffered immensely, it is difficult to compare it to the mag-

nitude of MacDonald's suffering because
MacDonald lost far more than his freedom. He lost his entire family.

August 29, 1979, was the first night
and no doubt one of the worst nights
Jeffrey MacDonald has spent in prison. He
had just experienced the shock of a
guilty verdict, handcuffs and chains, and
finally, arrival at the Federal
Correctional Institute at Butner, North
Carolina. The guard maintained a suicide
watch during his first night there,
shining a light through the food slot of
the cell's steel door every fifteen
minutes.

Of this whole terrifying situation,
MacDonald wrote: "If there is a heaven,
as Colette and Kim always felt, I'm sure
that Colette, Kim, Kristy and our unborn
son are there now. What must they be
saying as they look down on this
insanity? Does their new status give
them infinite patience and understanding
of mere mortals' errors and procedures?
Or are they as sick of all this as I am?
I wished I was with them now, wherever it
might be."

During MacDonald's second night at
Butner a prisoner in his cell block set
fire to a mattress and smoke billowed
throughout the area. Unbelievably, the
guard on duty announced to MacDonald that
the rules required two guards for every
inmate they let out, and since he was the
only guard on duty, he couldn't let
anyone out. After MacDonald let him know
that there would shortly be eight inmates

and one guard dead of smoke inhalation if they weren't let out quickly, more guards materialized and they were moved to a "nonsmoking area."

For the next several weeks, MacDonald was taken from prison to jail to prison as he made his way to the Federal Penitentiary at Terminal Island, which is near his home in Huntington Beach, California.

In the Atlanta Federal Penitentiary, MacDonald was placed in solitary confinement "for his own safety". Here he was taken by surprise when a trustee unlocked his cell door and wandered in during the middle of the night. He had come to let MacDonald know that they would take care of him and to "be cool". Later on, a sympathetic guard further clued MacDonald in on the reality of the place. "We got a bunch of assholes here, Doc," warned the guard. "They'll cut your throat for a nickel, a quarter or just a line in the newspaper. Now when you get in the clothing line, take an extra shirt and keep it wrapped around your left arm and get some extra newspapers and put them inside your shirt as protection, and when you walk down the hall, always keep one shoulder near the wall so you only have to defend one side."

After the Atlanta Penitentiary, the Jackson, Mississippi jail was a pleasant surprise. Instead of the "southern justice" MacDonald and his group feared, they encountered "southern hospitality," clean quarters and home cooking, by the wife of one of the guards.

The Texarkana, Texas, prison was a different story. There were episodes of violence during MacDonald's short stay there. Fortunately they did not involve him. One incident concerned the stabbing of an inmate and a 45 minute wait for paramedics to get inside the gate to treat him. When other inmates rattled their cell bars in protest of this situation, the guards pulled them out of their cells one by one and beat them.

Next stop, El Reno, Oklahoma. Here, MacDonald spent five days in a former reform school recently converted into a penitentiary with a high percentage of young convicts and a reputation for prison yard violence.

When MacDonald finally arrived at Terminal Island, he was made a clerk in the office which handled the training of guards. Despite the fact that Terminal Island is a forbidding gray fortress that comes nowhere near the standards of cleanliness and safety MacDonald under-standably desires, he prefers it to the more modern, civilized prisons like FCI Bastrop and FCI Phoenix because he is closest to home here. To MacDonald, this means frequent visits with family and friends and close communication with his lawyers.

The 4th Circuit Court decision overturning MacDonald's guilty verdict because his rights to a speedy trial had been violated, was a long time in coming. Then it was still another month before he

was released on $100,000 bail at the Los
Angeles Federal Building on August 21,
1980. He then quickly began to rebuild
his life. Little did he know that, though
his condominium and friends were waiting
for him, as well as his position at St.
Mary Medical Center, again, the worst
was yet to come.

A little less than a year and a half
later, on March 31, 1982, shortly after
he was made Emergency Director at St.
Mary Medical Center, the Supreme Court
ruled 6-3 that MacDonald's rights to a
speedy trial had not been violated--des-
pite the fact that much of the physical
evidence had been lost or destroyed.
Despite the fact that witnesses suffered
from loss of memory over the nine-year
span of time from when the crimes were
committed until the trial. And despite
some witnesses simply vanishing alto-
gether.

Within hours of the decision, the
FBI picked up MacDonald and returned him
to the penitentiary at Terminal Island.
During the short ride from Huntington
Beach to Terminal Island, one of the FBI
agents recounted to MacDonald the race
between the various law enforcement
agencies to re-arrest him. It is frankly
amazing to me that the FBI "won." I say
this on account of two recent incidents.
The first took place during an inaugural
dinner given by President Reagan's close
friends, the Jorgensens, who live near
us. While winding my way home, children
in tow, we slowly negotiated a blind

curve, just before approaching the Jor-
gensen's home, only to find a man standing square in the middle of the street
as if waiting calmly to be run over.

As I came to a grinding halt inches
from him, he approached the car and
flashed his FBI identification at me. I
informed him that even small children
were taught not to stand in the middle of
the street, particularly on a blind
curve. I asked him why his mother never
taught him the most basic "street wise"
rules. He replied that I was going too
fast, but one of my sons quickly set him
straight, stating that I was going 5
miles under the speed limit of 15 miles
per hour. Then I proceeded to ask him
how he intended to take care of the
Reagans when he couldn't take care of
himself. Red-faced and flustered, he
impatiently waved me on.

The second incident was related to
me by my brother, who was at the time a
deputy sheriff in Santa Barbara. It
began with a frantic phone call to him at
about 6:00 a.m. one morning from an FBI
agent. The agent stated that the sheriff
had designated my brother to lead the
Reagan "procession" from the Santa
Barbara airport to the Reagans' ranch
about an hour's drive further north. For
a reason which will no doubt remain
forever unexplained, the FBI had not
notified the Sheriff's Department of
Reagan's pending arrival. Hence, Reagan
was kept waiting in a cold damp airport
hangar for almost 30 minutes while my

brother threw on his clothes and drove his patrol car the 20 miles from Montecito, a small suburb on the south side of Santa Barbara, to Goleta, on the north side of Santa Barbara, where the airport is situated.

My brother had never led the presidential procession to the ranch before, but had recently become politically "in" with the public as well as the Sheriff's Department for his success in catching a group of thugs. They had been stealing Fuerte avocados off trees and selling them at a very low price to restaurants, and at a very high profit for themselves. My brother had no idea what the route was supposed to be, so he just drove to the ranch taking the only route he knew, and nobody complained.

The FBI did manage to deliver MacDonald safely to his horrifying destination: the Terminal Island Penitentiary. Here the survival routine of workouts, baseball, football, visits from his lawyer, family and friends began; with the highlights of each week being visits from his fiancee Randi Dee Markwith.

During July and August, "Washington Post" columnist Jack Anderson interviewed MacDonald and produced a documentary which concentrated on the outrageous government cover-ups in his case, and the government's tremendous efforts to keep MacDonald from receiving Freedom of Information Act material. Shortly after the documentary aired and several

"Washington Post" articles ran on these
subjects, MacDonald was suddenly transferred 1,500 miles away to Bastrop,
Texas, (despite a Federal Bureau of
Prison's policy which states that inmates
are to be incarcerated as close to their
families as possible).

Many people believe that MacDonald
was moved from Terminal Island to the
Federal Correctional Institiute at Bastrop so that he would be less accessible
to the media. If this were the case, it
didn't work. The Associate Warden, who
handled the media at FCI Bastrop,
believed in obeying the Federal Bureau of
Prison's policy which allows inmates
access to the media. MacDonald was,
therefore, allowed to accept and reject
interviews almost at will.

All in all, 1982 was a treacherous,
energytaxing, emotionally draining year
for MacDonald. On the 16th of August, the
4th Circuit Court turned down Mac-
Donald's next appeal, finding that his
trial had been error free. This despite
the fact that Judge Dupree had refused
MacDonald access to the majority of the
physical evidence in his favor and had
pre-judged and ruled without jurisdiction
on other crucial evidence and court
procedures.

On August 27, MacDonald began the
long trek from Terminal Island to Bastrop, Texas, by way of Lompoc, California, i.e., Federal Bureau of Prison's
"logic" dictates one must go north before
being allowed to travel to a southerly

destination.

At Lompoc, Randi broke her engagement to MacDonald. Hence, during the short period of time between the end of March and his six week stay at Lompoc, the Supreme Court ruled against him, he was put back in prison, he lost an appeal to the 4th Circuit Court and he lost his fiancee.

Shortly after the breakup, MacDonald began his tedious journey from Lompoc south to Bastrop, Texas, which is near Austin. MacDonald arrived at FCI-Bastrop on October 20, and found the facilities to be satisfactory for what they were. The next day he immediately began his survival routine - lifting weights, running, competitive sports, writing letters to his family, friends and supporters, keeping up with medicine and above all, working on his case.

In early 1983, MacDonald finally began to obtain his Freedom of Information Act material, thanks to pressure from Jack Anderson, retired FBI agent Ted Gunderson, the House of Representatives and the Senate. From this material, it was discovered that key physical evidence which supported MacDonald's recollection of the crimes had been suppressed by the government. This physical evidence also led to new witnesses, which combined, built a new case for MacDonald.

In addition to the new case, MacDonald had high hopes for the book about his life being written by Joe McGinniss, who had grown to become one of his closest friends. McGinniss had sympathized with MacDonald, given advice to his defense team and professed loyalty to MacDonald, his family and friends.

In the early fall of 1983, when Mike Wallace informed him during a "60 Minutes" interview that "Fatal Vision" was an unfavorable book, it came as one of the supreme shocks of all time to MacDonald.

After reading "Fatal Vision" and viewing the "60 Minutes" episode on the case, I knew that something was very wrong--exactly what, I didn't know, but I decided to do my best to find out.

The first time I visited MacDonald at Bastrop was on Friday, January 13, 1984. It felt strange of course, to be in a prison, but like the many other friends and members of the press who visited with him there, his lively conversation, combined with his surprisingly natural charm, allow one to quickly lose track of the surroundings.

There are times when you cannot help but be conscious that you are there. The first time is when you drive up Highway 95 from Elgin toward Bastrop and you see the big road sign that says "Federal Correctional Institute" with an arrow pointing left. Shortly after you turn in, there is a sign telling unauthorized persons to go no further. You continue on until you reach a parking lot, which is for all prison personnel and visitors (no horses allowed).

Next, you enter a reception area,

which is as stark a room as you will probably ever see. It contains a desk with a guard sitting behind it, a mini-switchboard where the majority of the incoming calls come through, (except for the chief warden who has his own private line) the electronic controls for the doors which lead out to the prison grounds, four or five plastic seats, a metal detector, and lockers for purses. Purses cannot be taken into the visiting room because you might be smuggling drugs or some yummy chocolate cake with a Magnum .45--or my preference, a '55 magnum of champagne, for the friend you are visiting.

After signing in at the desk and giving the number and unit of the person you are visiting, the guard calls the visiting room where the files are kept, to make sure you are authorized to visit. This being the case, a guard is called to escort you to the visiting room. Once you are there, the only other time you are conscious of being in prison is when visiting hours are over and you line up to be counted by the guard before leaving.

Life at FCI-Bastrop is certainly not as it is portrayed in the movies. The attractive dining area pictured in Chapter VIII is more appealing than many office cafeterias. The menu is varied and basically healthful, although MacDonald would probably argue that this isn't quite so. His chief complaint while at Bastrop was that because they got literally tons of free butter due to farm surpluses, almost every kind of food served was loaded with it. Another complaint involved a chef who put early peas in almost all the main dishes, giving them a chalky taste. All in all, however, the food was bearable. For MacDonald, it was being innocent and being at Bastrop that made life for him there about as unbearable as life can get.

There is a factory at FCI-Bastrop. Inmates who do not have money sent in and need to earn their $95.00 per month spending allotment want to work there because it pays more than other prison jobs. The factory manufactures helmets and ship-to-shore boat covers. The group of inmates whom I met working there were polite, pleasant, hard workers. Several of the men went out of their way to explain the workings of the factory to me. One nice older man from Iowa came over to tell me that he had just six months to go before being sent home and that he would never do anything bad again--he had learned his lesson.

After a supervisor told me about the superior safety conditions in the factory, the man next to me pointed out the burn he had received from one of the ovens. Perfect timing. When I mentioned that the horrible smell of plastic being melted down must cause a lot of cancer, I was told that they did have masks but that no one would wear them. Had MacDonald, with his ever present dedication to health worked in that factory, I have a feeling everyone would be wearing masks.

The gym at FCI-Bastrop is still relatively new and the staff and sports-minded residents are very proud of it. There is also a repair shop where one can learn how to repair motorcycles, cars, etc. The grounds are beautifully kept and if it weren't for the razor-wire fence, you'd think you were in a neighborhood park. When I mentioned this to the associate warden he reminded me that without freedom, nothing can be appreciated.

I discovered very quickly that even though MacDonald was locked up, he was still very much in command when it came to his case. He made full utilization of the methods of communication available to him. The most important was the telephone, because it was the closest thing to being on the other side of the fence.

The 1984-85 evidentiary hearings were planned on the phone. And when MacDonald was being portrayed as a murderer in the TV movie adaptation of "Fatal Vision," a fellow inmate picked up the telephone to communicate to the press that MacDonald was, during those very moments, saving a life. Much to the dismay of government prosecutors and his in-laws, a news bulletin stating, "MacDonald saves a life," flashed across the screen during the very moments they had counted on to convince millions he was a murderer.

The incident began when MacDonald was called by guards who had discovered that a man who had lost his appeal and had attempted to commit suicide had stopped breathing. MacDonald literally brought him back to life. Shortly after that, MacDonald almost lost his own life when someone attacked him while he was on the telephone with his back turned. Though FCI-Bastrop has a low level of violence, occasionally incidents like this happen. The violent inmate who had been mistakenly placed in this predominently "white collar" prison is now residing in Leavenworth.

MacDonald received decent medical treatment only because the associate warden had enough sense to send him to an excellent hospital in Austin. Medical facilities at Bastrop, as in most prisons, are next to non-existent.

The last time I visited MacDonald at Bastrop was two days after the October 7, 1985, oral arguments for MacDonald's 4th Circuit Court Appeal to overturn Judge Dupree's decision against a new trial. When I arrived at the prison, I was told that the associate warden, Larry Taylor, was down in the sewers. Since he had okayed this visit (because I was bringing in a camera to take pictures of MacDonald) I couldn't get in without him.

First I asked the guard at the desk if I could go down to the sewers and retrieve him. The answer was a horrified "No!" That being the case, I asked if they would please send a guard down to get him. After a call to a Lieutenant, who called a Captain, my request was approved and a guard was dispatched to the sewers. Out came Larry Taylor, who was apologetic and had MacDonald sent for immediately. While waiting, we discussed his case. I found that he had kept up with every aspect of it and knew exactly what MacDonald's options were at that point.

When MacDonald arrived, I took pictures of him for the book, the "MacDonald Newsletter," his family and friends. We discussed the oral arguments and our hopes for some good news soon. Not too long after this visit, MacDonald was suddenly transferred from Bastrop, Texas, to Phoenix, Arizona.

He called on December 19 to say that he was at the Federal Correctional Institute in El Reno and would be there until after the first of the year because the federal planes were "taking off" for the holidays. El Reno may not be a paradise as far as facilities go, but like FCI-Bastrop, a reasonable amount of communication was possible, and so it was bearable. MacDonald had originally requested the transfer to FCI-Phoenix about a year ago and I had always had a sense of foreboding, being a firm believer that the grass is not always greener. That certainly turned out to be the case at FCI-Phoenix. After being flown to Tucson, dumped in a drunk tank with no heat, driven by van to Phoenix, where he was put in the Maricopa County

Jail, he was finally taken to FCI Phoenix.

Everything there is allegedly better than at any other federal prison anywhere. The facilities are modern, the food good, and the staff reasonable to get along with, in most instances. Everything is better, except for the most important thing, communication. Each inmate is only allowed one 10-to-15 minute phone call per day, which must be reserved the day before. It has brought about an incredible amount of dissension, disruption and downright chaos in regard to MacDonald's case, particularly because of the extreme difficulty he has in reaching his lawyers, and they, him.

In addition to working on his case, working out and keeping in touch with friends and supporters, his job (everyone must have one) is as a dorm orderly. In describing it, he says, "I clean the dorm. And I take care of the pool tables and the chairs and vacuum and wax just like a housewife, only it's in a dorm for about 70 people...men." MacDonald goes on to say that, "Each day is spent pouring out enormous energy, keeping everything as normal as possible under the circumstances...

"People keep telling me that time heals wounds. They do not appear to be correct. I wonder how many of them lost what was dearest to them and then babbled on about time healing all wounds."

To mark the end of Dreyfus' fight

for freedom, he was designated Knight of the Legion of Honor in a ceremony honoring him at the Ecole Militaire, where twelve years earlier he had been stripped of all honor.

After the ceremony, Dreyfus answered shouts of "Long live Dreyfus!" with "Long live the Republic! Long live truth!" Dreyfus' wife Lucie, children Pierre and Jeanne, and his brother Mathieu were close by. Of them he stated that the highlight of the day was "the delicious embrace of all those I love, and for whom I had the courage to go on living."

MacDonald has lost his family, but he still has a life. When will he able to live it? The answer lies in the hands of all of us who believe in the pursuit of liberty and justice for all.

MR. PRESIDENT: HEAR MY PLEA!

11

PROLOGUE

Following, is MacDonald reliving the attack on his family and himself under hypnosis. (William S. Kroger, M.D., conducted the psychiatric-hypnotic interview of Dr. Jeffrey MacDonald in June of 1979. Dr. Kroger is an internationally known authority on medical hypnosis and psychosomatic medicine.)

"I'm reading ...It's Mickey Spillane ...It's almost 2 ...Two A.M ...I turn the FM off ...Get ready for bed ...Going to the bedroom ...Kristie is in bed ... Colette's on her left side ...She rolls over to her right side ...Kristie starts to move ...The bed's wet ...Kristie wet the bed ...I pick up Kristie and her bottle ...Bring her to her room ...Tuck her in ...She's okay ...I get a blanket ...Go to the couch ...After 2 ...It's late ...I lay down and go to sleep

"What's going on here? ...What the hell are you people doing in my house? ..What are you assholes doing here? ...I hear Kimmy ...I hear my wife ...I start to get up. ...What the ---- are you assholes doing here? ...I see a girl ...She says 'acid is rain ...acid is rain.' ...The black guy is going to hit me ...He's got something in his hand ...I'm trying to get up ...He does hit me ...On the head ...I'm back on the couch ...My head hurts ...I hear Colette ...I hear my wife ...'Jeff ...Jeff ...why ...why are they ...why are they doing this to me?' ...She's screaming, 'Jeff. Help me! Jeff stop them!'

"He's moving towards me ...I'm trying to get up ...The blanket is holding me down ...I'm trying to get up ...What the ---- are you assholes doing in my house? ...A girl's voice says, 'Acid is groovy, kill the pigs.' ...I said, 'What the ----, acid is groovy?' ...Some black ...A black guy standing there ...he's raising something ...I can't see it ...it's behind him ...He's raising something ...He's going to hit me ...I hear the girl say 'Acid is groovy, kill the pigs.' Colette is screaming. I said, 'Get the ---- out of here you assholes.'

"I hear Kimmy screaming, ...'Daddy, daddy!' ...I hear Kimmy. ...I say, 'Kimmy I'll help you. ...I'll help you, Kimmy.' ...Kimmy is ...'Daddy ...Daddy ... Daddy ...Daddy.'

"This ---- ---- is going to hit me

...It's behind his shoulder, behind his
right shoulder ...I'm pushing up ...I'm
pushing up with my right hand and my left
hand is up ...These asshole ---- ---- ,
what are they doing here? ...I've got to
move forward so the black guy can't hit
me so much ...It's little punches ...I
grab hold of one of them's shirt and pull
myself up ...The guy on the right ...I
grab his shirt ...I'm pulling myself up
...The creep in the middle ...the little
punk in the middle is punching me in the
chest ...He's a big doper, there's no
question about it...

"There's a girl between the two
white guys ...Acid is rain? ...I don't
understand this ...What the ---- are they
doing in my house? One guy is punching
me and the black guy is going to hit me
with a club ...He's trying to hit me
...My left arm hurts like crazy ...he hit
me in the left arm and shoulder ...He's
going to hit me again ...It's just
something swinging ..It hits me in the
left hand and the left arm and in the
left upper arm ...And it knocks me back
flat on the couch again.

"I've got to get up. I can't get up
...I can't help ...I can't help ...I've
got to get up ...I can't ...what the ----
is going on? ...I can't ...what is going
on ...I've got to get up ...I'm still on
the couch ...I've got to get up ...I'm
still trying to get up again now ...I'm
trying to get back up ...The blanket is
still up ...I'm trying to pull it off
with my right hand ...The guy on the

right is still punching me ...The black
guy swings again and this time I grab his
arm. I've got his arm! I reach over with
my right arm, and I've got his arm.

"He's got an army jacket on ...He's
got six stripes ...Three ...three V's on
the top and one rocker on the bottom
...It's black ...I can't see well ...it's
a green jacket and the rocker ...That's
all I see and I'm holding on to his lower
right arm and he's trying to jerk it out
...I've got his hand ...It's a weird
glove ...It's rough ...I ...I've got to
fight ...I've got to push this guy off
...I can't let him hit me in the head
with the club.

"Okay ...I've got it ...I've got his
hand ...They are worker rubber gloves
...Gardening gloves or dishwasher gloves
...Coarse ...They go up under the ...the
army jacket ...I can't see the fingers
...I have his hand ...His fingers are
wrapped behind the club ...It's a pretty
big hand ...Both my hands have his hand

"I'm getting punched in the head and
...and ...the right side of the head, the
right chest ...and the right arm ...They
are jerking me towards ...they are
jerking me towards the end of the couch
...I'm trying to jerk the club away from
this guy so I can use the club ...I'm
trying to jerk it away ...I'm jerking on
his hand and my left hand is sliding back
on the club ...I'm jerking ...Something's
in my way now ...There's something over
my head ...There's something they are
jerking on me you know ...and I'm pushing

on them and I'm jerking on the club all
at once ...Something is in my way ...I
can't push back at the two white guys
...I can't push back ...well ...Something
is over my hands ...My hands are all
bound up ...I can't pull as well ...I
can't push the white guys as well ...and
I can't pull on the club as well ...They
are wrapped in something.

"Can't get up ...It's hard to get up
now ...I am trying to get up ...Can't get
the ---- blanket off my feet ...It's an
afghan ...Can't get my feet out.

"He's going to hit me again ...I
can't let him hit me in the head again
...He's going to swing at me again ...His
arms are behind his right shoulder
...He's going to hit me again ...He
...swinging something at me ...He hit my
left arm and my left head ...I've got his
arm ...I'm holding on to his arm so he
can't hit me again. ---- head hurts
...What the ---- is going on here? Who
are these guys? ...I ...I can't figure
out what is going on ...Why ...why is my
wife screaming?

"I've got his arm ...He's trying to
jerk it away ...I'm sliding off his arm
...If I let go, he is going to hit me
again ...I'm sitting up ...I'm being
jerked towards the end of the couch
...Two guys are punching me ...They are
pulling me to the end of the couch ...I'm
trying to push them away ...I've got one
guy's jacket and I've still got the guy's
arm ...They're pulling me to the end of
the couch by my shirt ...I can't see them

...I'm all ...I'm all bound up ...My pajama top is all around my arms ...It's around my hands ...I use it partially as a shield ...He's going to hit me again.

"They are punching me in the chest. I've got a terrific pain in my right chest ...I see this girl between the two white guys. She's skinny ...She looks wasted ...She's standing there, between the two white guys ...There's a light on her face ...She's blonde. She's saying, 'Acid is groovy, kill the pigs, acid is groovy, kill the pig ...Acid and rain.'...Flickering light on her face...

They're punching me in the chest ...I'm trying to push away now ...I've got a pain in my right chest ...I said 'What the ---- are you doing?' ...I'm trying to push them away ...My arms are bound up...My arms are all wrapped up ...I can't do anything ...I'm still trying to kick the ------ blanket off my feet and my hands are bound up! ...I ...I ...can't do anything! ...I'm trying to push them away!

My hands aren't free ...They're not free and I can't do anything well ...They're punching me in the chest ...I've got a terrific pain in my right chest ...My head hurts ...I've got someone's hand ...My hands are all bound up but I've got ...I've got a hand ...I saw a blade ...The ---- pain isn't a punch ...I got stabbed ...Short, small knife ...it's been pulled back ...I'm going to get stabbed again ...I can't get my hands free ...I've got someone's arm

...I don't think it's the same arm ...I
think the guy's going to stab me again
...And the black guy's still got the
club.

My head isn't clear ...I've got a
------ pain in my head ...They are
punching me in the right chest ...Both
guys ...Both guys ...This guy's bigger
...This guy's bigger than the guy in the
middle ...I think I've got his arm
...He's trying to jerk his arm away
...I'm trying to pull it away ...I'm
trying to pull it away ...I've got both
his arms ...He's trying to stab me
...There's a blade ...I can't see a blade
...He's trying to jerk his arms away ...I
know he ..I know it ...I know he's
trying to pull his hands away ...Someone
is punching me ...I've got one arm
...I've got one arm ...They are punching
me.

Stomach ...stomach ...pain ...I
can't keep ...get a good hold ...This
guy's left arm ...I've got ...I'm trying
to hold his left arm ...he's trying to
jerk it away ...He's bigger ...He's
stronger ...I can see this bigger guy
...He's bigger ...He's bigger and
stronger ...I've got his left arm ...He's
bigger and stronger ...His hands are
slippery ...They feel slippery ...I've
got his left arm ...I know he's going to
stab me if I let go ...I can't keep
holding on ...He's pulling his left arm
away ...I can't keep pulling away ...My
------ head hurts.

I can't keep holding ...My ------

pajama top is wrapped all around ...I can't free my arms! ...I can't keep his arm away and I can't get a good grip ...Someone is punching me in the abdomen and the chest and I can't keep pushing away ...----! Someone hit me with a club ...In the left arm ...I don't know what to do ...I'm trying to push them away ...I've got to get my hands free! ...I've got to keep them away! ...I'm still pulling ...Still trying to push them away ...Acid is groovy, kill the pig ...It's all I hear ...No sounds ...Acid is groovy, kill the pig.

They're going to kill me! ...I'm trying to push them away ...The arm is slipping away ...I've got the hand ...I can't keep on long ...It's slippery ...I can't keep holding on! ...It's slippery ...It feels wet ...I can't keep my hands ...don't have a good grip ...My pajama top is sliding over ...I can't keep holding on! ...I can't do it! ...He's jerking his arm away. ----! ...I'm sliding forward!

I'm sliding forward ...I'm sliding forward. I...see ...I see ...A knee ...See a bare knee ...Wh... wh... My arms! They're so heavy! ...I can't get them up. I saw a knee ...Wh ...Why ...I can't tell ...What the ---- is happening? ...I see ...the top ...the top of a boot ...the boot ...Right after the knee ...Bare leg ...top of a boot ...White leg ...Top of a boot ...high boot ...Light brown ...looks wet ...looks wet ...Light brown, it looks wet ...Girl's leg ...What the ---- ...I can't see ...What is ...my head hurts! My ------ head!

I can't! My head! ...I can't ...I'm moving ...I ...I got hit in the head ...It's dark ...One split second ...One split second it's dark ...The steps ...One spli ...split second ...Steps ...coming up. Steps coming up. At my waist!

My hands are under me ...I can't get my hands out ...I can't get them out ...My hands are under my chest ...My chest hurts ...I'm on the floor ...My head hurts ...My head hurts ...I can't ...I can't think! ...I feel cold ...On the floor ...My arms are under me ...Face down ...They are folded up under my chest ...Pajama tops are on my wrist and hands ...I smell wax on the floor ...Wooden floor, waxed.

My teeth are chattering ...My head hurts ...I'm freezing ...My head hurts ...I see ...can't clear my head ...I can smell the floor ...Remembering I heard screams ...It's quiet ...I can't hear anything except my teeth ...I'm getting up ...I'm going to go see Colette ...I go down the hallway ...My head hurts like crazy and I feel like I'm going to pass out ...I'm in the hallway ...I feel like I can't breathe.

My head hurts ...in front of the bathroom ...just walking into the bedroom. There's something on the floor ...I can't see well ...Colette ...She's leaning against the green chair ...Can't get the pajama top off my hands ...I'm

trying to find some light ...I've got the
light on ...I've got to get the pajama
top off ...I'm pulling on it to get it
off my hands ...It's coming off ...off,
yes ...

Looking at Colette ...She's bloody
...There's a knife in her chest ...I pull
the knife out ...I lay her on the floor
...I give her mouth to mouth ...The air
is coming out of her chest ...The air is
coming out of her chest ...It's not
working ...Checking for pulse ...She
doesn't have a pulse ...I remember Kimmy
was screaming ...I got up to go see
Kimmy. She looks bloody too ...She's my
little girl ...She looks funny ...She
looks dead ...I've checked her left
carotid ...No pulse ...I tilt her head
back ...I ...I'm giving Kimmy mouth to
mouth ...I can't see if her chest is
rising ...It doesn't ...it sounds like
bubbles ...I think there's bubbles in her
...in her neck ...I can't figure out
what's going on ...Can't figure out why
...why she's ...why she's this way.

I've got to see if Kristen
...Kristie, you'd better be okay ...She's
across the hall ...She looks pale
...She's in her bed ...She's facing me
...She looks pale ...She doesn't ...she
doesn't look good ...She doesn't look
like she's breathing ...I have to tilt
her head up to feel her pulse ...Her
right corotid ...I can't feel a pulse
...I have to give her mouth to mouth ...I
don't think her chest is rising though
...I don't think it's working on Kristie

either ...Going back to Colette
      She looks terrible ...She's got
blood all over ...I check for a femoral
pulse ...I can't believe ...I can't find
a pulse ...It's my wife! ...Covering her
chest ...Something from the green chair
...I can't see what it is ...Seems like a
towel ...I picked up my pajama top ...I
put it on Colette ...I go to the phone.
      I pick it up ...I dial 'O' ...An
operator ...'Yes?' ...'This is Captain
MacDonald ...I need help ...People are
dying ...We've been stabbed ...544 Castle
Drive ...Hurry! ...There's people been
stabbed ...We're dying ...Send M.P.'s and
ambulances ...Send help ...We need help'
...She says is it on the post or off-post
...I don't know ...I can't figure out why
she asked me that ...I said it's on post
...I threw the phone down...
      Standing at Colette's feet ...I
notice door is opened ...the back door
...Out ...outside door ...It's cold out
...And wet ...I looked around to see if I
could see the people ...Dark ...My feet
feel wet ...I can see the grass ...Winter
grass ...It's not green ...I can see the
sidewalk ...It looks wet ...Can't see
anyone ...I can't figure out what's going
on ...I can't figure out how to help
Colette ...I walk back down the hallway
...I don't know ...I don't know what to
do ...Standing in the hallway ...I can't
figure out what...what ...I can't figure
it out ...My chest is hurting ...Can't
breathe well ...Can't ...I can't clear my
head.

I look down at my chest. I can see
my chest bubbling a little. I go in the
bathroom, I look in the mirror, look at
my head. The bruise at the left temple
...Skin is broken a little ...about two
inches across ...Doesn't look like it
feels ...There's blood smeared on my
forehead ...There's blood around my lips
...on my hands ...it's all over both
hands ...My stomach ...There's a little
bit around my chest.

I wash my hands ...Go back to
Colette ...I picked up my pajama top
...to see if her chest looks as bad as I
first saw it ...It looks horrible ...
She's...there's wounds all over her ...I
hugged her ...I told her ...the kids
would be okay ...I told her the kids
would be okay. I'm kneeling next to her.
I put the pajama top back. I decide to
check the kids one more time ...I can't
believe it.

I've got to get up...I can't breathe
well though ...My head hurts...I get
up...I have to push myself up ...I've got
to...got to check Kimmy ...Kimmy is my
little girl ...I've got to go see her
...I go back to see her ...I give her
mouth to mouth ...Kimmy is limp ...Kimmy
looks terrible ...I pick her up ...My
left hand is under her shoulder
...picking her up towards me ...My right
arm is under her neck ...I give Kimmy
mouth to mouth ...It doesn't feel right
...There's no resistance to her breathing
...The air must be escaping ...It must be
coming out her neck or chest ...I put her

back ...She's got ...she's got wounds in her upper chest or neck ...It's not going to work ...I can't help her ...Mouth to mouth won't work ...Check her pulse ...I checked her femoral pulse ...There's no pulse ...I pick her up ...pick up her bed clothes ...Her bed clothes ...And lay them on her ...And go see Kristie.

I have to see Kristie ...Kristie has to be okay ...She's in her bed ...I'm in Kristie's room ...I just patted her head and told her it would be okay ...I told Kristie that ...everything would ...would be okay ...I'd get help ...She'd be okay ...I put my right hand behind her back ...She ...I reach across her and checked her right carotid ...There's no pulse ...Straighten out her blankets ...Went to call for help ...I'm in the kitchen ...pickup the phone ...Someone's on the phone ...woman said 'Is this Captain MacDonald?' ...'Yes' ...I started yelling at her ...'People have been stabbed ...We need help ...we need police, M.P.'s ambulances, send the ambulances ...Hurry! ...We're all dying' ...'I'll connect you' she says ...A male voice says 'It's sergeant someone.' ...Can't make it out ...I say send ...send help ...I said we need help ...We need everything ...Ambulances, M.P.'s, police, Help! We're dying we need help! Jesus Christ send some help! 544 Castle Drive. He was yelling to someone ...Make that ASAP to Womack ...I dropped the phone ...I'm standing there.

It's quiet ...looking at my hands

...my head hurts ...I can't clear my head
...I can't ...I can't ...I can't think
of what to do ...My head is pounding ...I
can't ...reach up to touch the back of my
head to feel why it's pounding so much
...I have ...I have to ...go be with
Colette ...In ca ...In case I can help
when the ambulance comes ...I'm laying
next to Colette ...That's it.

Someone is giving me mouth to mouth.
They are blowing air in my mouth ...It's
harder to breathe but I can breathe so I
am going to push them away ...I started
pushing them away ...There's a bunch of
people ...They are all over me ...A bunch
of M.P. helmets over me ...Shiny helmets
...White stripe ...Lots of people yelling
and screaming ...He said 'what happened?'
I said check my wife ...Help me! ...Help
my kids ...But please ...check my wife
and kids ...Please! ...He said 'you'll be
okay ...everyone was yelling and
screaming ...Christ there were 15 people
yelling and screaming ...what happened?
Who did it? Where are they? How many
were there? What happened? Jesus
Christ, don't move that! Don't touch
her! Put it down! Put it down! Check
the other rooms! Put that down you
asshole! ...Everyone is yelling ...The
guy over me ...he said 'what happened?'
He said 'are you a doctor?' ...someone
said 'he's a doctor.' ...This guy said
'are you a doctor?' ...I said yeah, I'm a
Captain ...he said 'what happened?' I
looked at my wife ...Jesus Christ, look
at my wife! ...He said 'it will be okay,

relax, we'll help you.' ...he was trying
to help me. He was pushing me back down.
I was laying next to Colette. He was
pushing me down but my head was on her
shoulder ...I didn't want my head to be
on her shoulder ...I ...I wanted to get
up and tell them what to do to help ...I
said help my kids.

Someone said 'Jeez, Jesus Christ,
the kids are ...they're just like this.'
I said help them. He said 'it's okay,
they'll be okay, we're all checking
them.' Someone said 'I got to call for
back-up ...this is to ------ big for us.'
There's a lot of noise and people are
yelling 'get back-up' ...I can hear poun
...pounding footsteps ...He's trying to
push me down ...I'm trying to push him
away ...I didn't want to lay on Colette.
They have to help Colette ...I didn't
want to lay on her! ...I'm trying to push
off and I grab him by the shirt and he
drags me away ...He's trying to help me!
He pulls me away ...pulls me about a foot
away from Colette towards the doorway
...I said Gee ...Jesus you've got to do
mouth to mouth! ...No ...no one's doing
anything right ...Except the guy trying
to help me ...I'm okay ...I said help the
kids! ...He says 'the kids are okay.'
...I'm ...I'm trying to think ...they
didn't ...they didn't look okay to me
...they didn't look ...they didn't look
okay."

"My God! The drug abusers have
killed them...I warned Jeff to be

careful."
Major James Williams
Commanding Officer of
Captain Jeffrey R. MacDonald
--February 17, 1970

MR. PRESIDENT: HEAR MY PLEA!

In Emile Zola's "J'Accuse," Zola summarizes the injustices dealt Dreyfus in a statement directed to the President of France.

Following is a summary of the injustices dealt MacDonald in a statement directed to the President of the United States:

In the name of one nation, undivided, with liberty and justice for all, I ask you to put an end to the rampant injustices suffered by Dr. Jeffrey MacDonald, at the hands of desperate criminals, fraudulantly masquerading as honorable officials of our government.

I accuse CID investigators Franz J. Grebner, Robert Shaw and William F.Ivory of negligence and prejudice against Dr. Jeffrey MacDonald -- which inturn caused them to: lie, cover-up, lose and destroy evidence; allow the murderers of Dr. MacDonald's family to go free; and force Dr. MacDonald to suffer cruel and inhumane punishment for crimes he did not commit, after already suffering the tragic loss of his family.

Despite at least 45 items establishing the presence of intruders in the MacDonald home--12 unidentified fingerprints and 17 unidentified palm-prints not belonging to any friends or acquaintances of the MacDonald's or their children or any of the Army inves-tigators, M.P.'s and other personnel who were called to the scene of the crime; one strand of brown hair not identified as belonging to anyone in the MacDonald family, all of whom had blond hair; one jewelry box containing redish brown stains and unidentified finger and palmprints plus 8 missing items of jewelry; at least three weapons not identified as coming from the MacDonald home; candlewax foreign to candles found in the MacDonald home; a bloody syringe; and a broken backdoor lock--despite un-deniable evidence of intruders, inves-tigator's Grebner, Shaw and Ivory refused to acknowledge the presence of intruders and therefore did not preserve the majority of this evidence.

To add to this outrageous situation, investigators Grebner, Shaw and Ivory stated that they found no evidence of a struggle despite the CID's authorization to reimburse MacDonald for claims for loss and damages incurred during the crimes which covered 38 items from every room in the house and include numerous pieces of furniture, carpeting, linens, china and jewelry.

Whether through ignorance, neg-ligence and/or prejudice, investigators Grebner, Shaw and Ivory accused MacDonald of staging the crimes despite clear and

overpowering evidence of intruders, a
monsterous struggle leaving a bloodbath
of destruction everywhere and wounds,
some of which would have been impossible
to selfinflict due to the directionality
of the thrusts; and another of which a
doctor would have been highly unlikely to
selfinflict because it was in an area
where penetration could not be controlled
and injury to nearby vital organs would
have likely killed him.

Due to this ignorance, negligence
and/or prejudice, investigator's Grebner,
Shaw and Ivory failed to set up roadblocks, allowing the four assailants
MacDonald had accused to escape with
potential exculpatory evidence.

I accuse William Ivory of losing or
purposely hiding or destroying a piece of
skin found under Colette MacDonald's
fingernail which could have proven Mac-
Donald's innocence beyond any reasonable
doubt.

I accuse William Ivory of improperly
preserving MacDonald's pajama top, which
could have proved him innocent had blood
not seeped through layers of fabric after
having been recklessly stuffed into a
plastic bag.

Grebner, Ivory and Shaw are not
worthy of our Army, which is one of our
country's most exalted sites of freedom
and truth, of honor and devotion toward
liberty and justice for all.

I accuse FBI scientist Paul Stombaugh of being a small-minded, selfish
man who abused his power and dishonored

the FBI by lying, cheating and persecuting Jeffrey MacDonald in order to preserve his image of success.

I accuse Paul Stombaugh of withholding the FBI's blood-typing results from MacDonald's defense because these results were different from the CID's blood-typing and corroborated MacDonald's recollection of the crimes and the crime scene.

I accuse Paul Stombaugh of covering up the invalidity of the prosecution's theory on how MacDonald allegedly killed each member of his family by keeping the FBI's blood-typing results hidden from the jury.

I accuse Paul Stombaugh of taking the holes in MacDonald's pajama top, which actually match certain of MacDonald's wounds, and which support his recollection of using it as a shield against his attackers after it became entrapped around his wrists--to create a false theory in which MacDonald stabbed through the pajama top to wound Colette 21 times, which established 48 holes in the pajama top, which makes no sense at all, particularly since many of the holes contradicted the directionality of the thrusts of the weapons; "weapons," please note, indicates more than one weapon, which indicates more than one assailant, which supports MacDonald's description of four assailants, all of whom knew each other, and three of whom have confessed to the crimes, and are corroborated by over thirty-five additional witnesses.

I believe that Stombaugh created this false theory in order to take advantage of the jurors' lack of technical forensic knowledge by confusing them with complicated explanations for the purpose of distorting clear, simple evidence of MacDonald's innocence into brutally misleading elements of guilt.

Paul Stombaugh is a disgrace to the FBI, which not only Americans but God-fearing people the world over, count on to defend them in their search for life, liberty and the pursuit of happiness.

I accuse Justice Department lawyer, Victor Worheide, now deceased, of disgracing the legal profession and the Department of Justice by using Dr. MacDonald's Grand Jury hearings as a prosecutorial tool rather than an investigative tool to serve justice. Worheide invited FBI and CID laboratory technicians to present their so-called "Pajama Top," "Fiber," and "Blood" theories to the Grand Jury without ever allowing the Grand Jury to hear the Article 32 Hearing defense testimony on these subjects, which had previously exonerated MacDonald of the crimes.

Worse, the four assailants MacDonald described, were not asked to testify before the Grand Jury, despite Col. Rock, the presiding officer of the Article 32 Hearing, ordering appropriate civilian authorities to investigate those MacDonald had accused.

These brief examples of Worheide's

outrageous conduct demand an extensive
and detailed review of the legal
standards practiced throughout our Justice Department to prevent further
atrocities from occurring.

I accuse James Blackburn, Assistant
United States Attorney, and Brian Murtaugh, Justice Department Attorney at
the time of MacDonald's 1979 trial, of
turning the legal profession and the
Department of Justice into a political
forum, which served to trample upon all
the principles of law and justice which
serve to make our country great.

I accuse Blackburn and Murtaugh of
collaborating with Stombaugh to present
MacDonald's 1979 trial jury with fraudulent forensic theories in order to convict MacDonald of crimes he did not commit with the motive of protecting the
government informants who did kill Mac-
Donald's family, and of furthering their
own careers.

I accuse Blackburn and Murtaugh of
refusing MacDonald's forensic expert, Dr.
John Thornton, access to the MacDonald
home for the purpose of studying the
evidence.

I accuse Blackburn and Murtaugh of
allowing MacDonald's step-father in-law,
Fred Kassab, access to the MacDonald home
during which time he mishandled crucial
evidence.

I accuse Blackburn and Murtaugh of
holding ex parte meetings with Judge
Dupree and of collaborating with Judge
Dupree against MacDonald by withholding

critical evidence from the defense, including a 13-volume government report
which substantiates MacDonald's recollection of the crimes and by disallowing
the jury to hear testimony from seven key
witnesses to the murders.

I accuse Blackburn and Murtaugh of
collaborating with "Fatal Vision" author,
Joe McGinniss, to present false statements about the evidence in an attempt to
convince the public of MacDonald's guilt.
Blackburn and Murtaugh have displayed a
contempt for the law and human values so
strong, that if nurtured, could literally
kill the very foundation of law, order
and justice upon which our country is
built.

I accuse Judge Franklin Dupree of
totally ignoring ethics and his duty to
be an impartial judge and instead taking
on the role of prosecutor and persecutor
of MacDonald—displaying acts of extreme
prejudice and monstrous partiality against MacDonald, as well as a total
disrespect for the laws of our land.

I accuse Judge Dupree of withholding
every piece of crucial evidence in Mac-
Donald's favor from the jury.

Judge Dupree ruled 0 for 24 in favor
of MacDonald's pre-trial and trial
motions, the majority of which involved
the presentation of evidence to the jury.
On the other hand, Judge Dupree ruled in
favor of 7 out of 8 of the prosecutions'
pre-trial and trial motions. In addition, Judge Dupree held ex parte meetings with the prosecution in order to

collaborate on how to obtain a guilty verdict from the jury.

I accuse Judge Dupree of breaking a legal agreement with the defense not to use a psychiatric report from two psychiatrists who had, unknown to the defense, previously acted as government agents in the case--unless the defense's psychiatric report was also admitted as evidence. Judge Dupree refused to allow the jury to hear MacDonald's positive psychiatric report, yet used the psychiatric report by government agents as his reason for refusing MacDonald bail, thereby blatantly ignoring the agreement and any semblance of law and order.

I accuse Judge Dupree of jury tampering and prejudice against blacks because he told all the prospective black jurors except one (the token), to go home and "help their daddys pick the tobacco."

I accuse Judge Dupree of swaying the jury against MacDonald. In addition to withholding all the crucial evidence supporting MacDonald's recollection of the crimes, Judge Dupree endeared himself to the jury by complimenting them and sympathizing with them and then making his disdain for the defense obvious by expressions of boredom, impatience and distaste.

I accuse Judge Dupree of refusing to let another judge hear the case despite his son-in-law being one of MacDonald's chief prosecutors, which is an unlawful conflict of interest and adds further to his blatant and vicious prejudice against

MacDonald.

The conduct Judge Dupree displayed at Jeffrey MacDonald's 1979 trial is an imperishable monument of naive audacity. As a judge and as a human being, Franklin Dupree is simply a miserable failure.

As Dreyfus loved and cherished France, Mr. President, Jeffrey MacDonald loves and cherishes America.

As Dreyfus rose to heroism through his leadership, protection and support of French ideals, MacDonald rose to heroism in America through his leadership, protection and support of American ideals--not just as an Army Captain, but as a doctor who, never content with present vistas of medicine, has continuously dedicated himself to future aspirations. Through his perseverance, MacDonald became one of the dominant forces in the development of our country's emergency and trauma systems, that today save millions of useful and treasured lives.

Even while in prison, Jeffrey MacDonald continues to dedicate himself to humanity through medicine: most recently, with his life-saving airway study, published in "The Annals of Emergency Medicine."

Mr. President: How much suffering must one American hero--who believes in the virtues of his country, and who religiously practices them despite monumental hardships--be allowed to endure?

Jeffrey MacDonald has lost his family. He has been attacked by those

who killed his family. He has been
viciously attacked in prison. He has
been humiliated with handcuffs and leg
irons, and with cries of hatred and in-
sults. He has sustained physical and
moral ordeals beyond life's worst night-
mares.

Though I wish his persecutors mercy,
I plead with you for their cesspools of
immorality to be purged of decay...and I
plead for your intervention in obtaining
freedom for Jeffrey MacDonald so that he
may see the rewards of his fantastic
courage and invincible convictions by
being restored to his rightful place in
life.

ACKNOWLEDGEMENTS

I would like to thank my husband, Roger, and our sons, R. J. and Clay for supporting me and encouraging me in the quest for exoneration and freedom for my friend, now their friend, Jeffrey MacDonald. They have given up many pleasures in the past few years, but I believe that we, both individually and as a family, have gained enormously from our experience.

Can I ever thank Jeffrey MacDonald enough for being Jeffrey MacDonald? I doubt it. Despite our often stormy relationship, there is an understanding, and so follows an every-growing closeness that, though sometimes marred by those who seek to benefit from its injury, continues to grow stronger through the knowledge gained by each of these experiences. There is a bond of truth and friendship between us that flourishes more so with the survival of each obstacle.

I have always believed in the Chinese proverb, "A picture is worth a thousand words," and I would like to thank Jeff's Mother, Dorothy (Perry) MacDonald for providing me with thousands of words through the pictures of Jeff's family and friends, which she so generously shared with me and has allowed me in turn to share with you, the reader.

To Jay MacDonald, thank you for providing me with a history of Jeff's life and case, without which I could not

have accurately written many parts of
this book.

Brian O'Neill should be thanked, not
just by me, but by all Americans in
search of justice. As Jeff has brought
the dying back to life through medicine
with his enormous determination and
efforts, so has O'Neill brought, through
law with his enormous determination and
efforts, a dying legal case about a
horrifying injustice, back to life. The
case has not been won yet, but thanks to
Brian O'Neill's leadership and his faith
in Jeffrey MacDonald and the law, there
is hope.

I would like Harold Friedman to know
how much I appreciate his support through
thick and thin, his bright ideas, and
most of all his wise advice.

Sincere thanks to Dennis Eisman for
his sensitivity and thoughtfulness in
relaying to me how refreshing it was for
him to find someone on this case who
spoke their true feelings.

Last, but certainly not least, I
would like to thank Ray Shedlick for
patiently educating me in the field of
forensics, and for his forceful support
during the inception of the "MacDonald
Newsletter."

The following exhibits were given to SP4 Joseph J. B ARBATO, US Army CI Lab, for analysis. His results are as follows:

EXHIBIT	DESCRIPTION	RESULTS
7-1	Urine sample from Captain MacDonald	No narcotics or dangerous drugs
7-2	Blood sample from Captain MacDonald	No narcotics or dangerous drugs

The following exhibit was given to the US Army Hospital at Fort Gordon, GA., for blood-alcohol analysis. The results are as follows:

EXHIBIT	DESCRIPTION	RESULTS
7-2	Blood sample from Captain MacDonald	0.150 mg/ml ethyl alcohol: not under influence of alcohol